# STONEWALL JACKSON'S 1862
## VALLEY CAMPAIGN

# STONEWALL JACKSON'S 1862 VALLEY CAMPAIGN

## WAR COMES TO THE HOMEFRONT

JONATHAN A. NOYALAS
Series Editor Douglas Bostick

THE
History
PRESS

Published by The History Press
Charleston, SC 29403
www.historypress.net

*Cover image*: *Shenandoah Autumn* by Mort Künstler, © 2003 Mort Künstler, Inc., www.mkunstler.com.

First published 2010
Second printing 2013

Manufactured in the United States

ISBN 978.1.59629.793.7

Noyalas, Jonathan A.
Stonewall Jackson's 1862 Valley Campaign : war comes to the homefront / Jonathan A.
Noyalas.
p. cm.
Includes bibliographical references and index.
ISBN 978-1-59629-793-7
1. Shenandoah Valley Campaign, 1862. 2. Jackson, Stonewall, 1824-1863--Military
leadership. I. Title.
E473.7.N69 2010
973.7'32--dc22
2010039246

*Dedicated to my wife Brandy—words can never express my love.*

# CONTENTS

# PREFACE

From the time the Civil War's guns fell silent in the spring of 1865 until the present century, each generation—perhaps taking heed of Voltaire's advice that each generation needs to rewrite history because each one ponders new historical questions—has chronicled the Civil War's drama. While future generations will undoubtedly recast the conflict in their own terms, as the Civil War's 150th anniversary approaches historians today also have a great chance to educate the wider public about our nation's epic struggle and its role as the pivotal, defining moment of our American republic. This book is written with that intention in mind.

Since the spring of 1862, Stonewall Jackson's Valley Campaign has captivated people around the world. The campaign's popularity has charmed historians for decades. Scholars such as James I. Robertson Jr.—who happened to be my thesis advisor during my graduate school days at Virginia Tech—Robert Tanner, Peter Cozzens, Robert K. Krick, Gary Ecelbarger and Brandon H. Beck (my undergraduate mentor) have investigated various aspects of Jackson's life and his famed campaign in the Shenandoah that played a crucial role in the Confederacy's military operations during the first half of 1862. This volume—intended to bring Jackson's Valley Campaign to life in a more succinct fashion for individuals with varying interests in the Civil War—builds on current scholarship, new research and new historical perspectives to offer some fresh insights into one of the Civil War's most storied campaigns: namely, how the campaign affected the valley's civilians, particularly Unionist sympathizers and African Americans; the role of art and other tools of historical memory in helping define the legacies of men such as Stonewall Jackson and General James Shields; and how, in defeat, Union veterans sometimes reflected positively on their involvement in Jackson's Valley Campaign.

In crafting this succinct volume, I have relied heavily on the primary accounts left by participants, some of which are in private collections and appear in this volume for the first time. Additionally, newspaper accounts and testimony in the Southern Claims Commission at the National Archives have aided me in crafting the campaign's story from the perspective of Shenandoah Valley civilians whose peaceful existence was interrupted by battles and military occupation.

Any book project is a tremendous undertaking and would not be possible without a supporting cast. The people I recognize have in some way contributed to this project but are in no way at fault for any of its errors: Dr. Brandon H. Beck, director emeritus of the McCormick Civil War Institute at Shenandoah University and the man who put Winchester's Civil War history on the map for a wider audience, has been a great friend and supporter of this project; Rebecca Ebert and the staff at the Stewart Bell Jr. Archives, Handley Regional Library in Winchester, Virginia, who always assist me on my visits to that repository and who have been active supporters of my publication projects; Dr. Irvin and Mrs. Nancy Hess, who always welcome my tours of Cross Keys and the Widow Pence Farm with enthusiasm; Elizabeth McClung, executive director of the Belle Grove House in Middletown, Virginia; Nicholas P. Picerno, my dear friend and tireless advocate of battlefield preservation in the valley and who opened up his collections once again for my use; the staff at the Valentine Richmond History Center, especially Meghan Holder, who assisted me with William Washington's painting *Stonewall Jackson Entering Winchester*; the staff of the R.W. Norton Gallery, especially Jerry Bloomer, for granting permission to reproduce L.M.D. Guillaume's painting *Stonewall Jackson at Winchester*; Patricia Stringfellow and the Jasper County Public Library in Rensselaer, Indiana; the staff at the Swem Library, College of William and Mary; the Virginia Historical Society, especially Dr. E. Lee Shepard; Dr. Joseph Whitehorne, my friend and colleague in the history department at Lord Fairfax Community College who shared his knowledge about the skirmish at Middletown in May 1862; and Karen Wisecarver, the interlibrary loan specialist at my institution, Lord Fairfax Community College, who went above and beyond the call of duty in tracking down multiple, obscure sources to support my research. Last but certainly not least, I would like to thank two people in my life who provide support that cannot be quantified: my son, Alexander Philip, who is a constant source of inspiration and joy, and my wife, Brandy, the love of my life and a fine historian and teacher, whose research assistance, advice and loving support have been invaluable.

# INTRODUCTION

Several months after the Civil War ended, John Trowbridge—a noted author of the time—toured Virginia's battlefields. As he rode in a train in Virginia's Shenandoah Valley, he witnessed war's devastating impact firsthand. "We passed through a region of country stamped all over by the devastating hell of war. For miles not a fence or cultivated field was visible."[1] In late 1865, Trowbridge witnessed the aggregate impact of incessant warfare on the valley's landscape and population. The Shenandoah Valley's role as the Breadbasket of the Confederacy—coupled with its transportation centers, its capacity to serve as an avenue of Confederate invasion into the North or a point from which Union troops could prevent such a movement and its ability to serve as a diversionary theater of operations for Confederate forces—made the Shenandoah Valley a magnet for both armies. Inventories of military action in the Shenandoah Valley make manifest the region's military significance. Most historians concur that the region experienced at least 325 engagements—battles, skirmishes or raids—during the conflict.[2] Although each engagement had various consequences in the war's larger scheme, no campaign dominates the American imagination more than Stonewall Jackson's 1862 Valley Campaign. Throughout the spring of 1862, Jackson's army marched nearly seven hundred miles, won five major battles and inspired an infant Confederate nation.

Although not as large as the 1864 Valley Campaign, which brought tremendous destruction to the area and cleared the valley of any substantial Confederate force, Jackson's 1862 Valley Campaign occurred at a time when the Confederacy was suffering setbacks on every other front—Forts Henry and Donelson were lost, Confederates were defeated at Shiloh, New Orleans was occupied by General Benjamin F. Butler, there was failure in Arkansas and General George B. McClellan's massive Army of the Potomac threatened Richmond. Jackson's campaign brought hope and inspiration to everyone in the Confederacy—soldiers and civilians alike. His achievements in the valley also aided the efforts of General Joseph E. Johnston to defend the Confederate capital by creating anxiety among war planners in Washington, D.C., who diverted troops away from McClellan and to the valley to deal with Jackson.

Undoubtedly one of the most celebrated campaigns in military history, the story of Jackson's 1862 Valley Campaign is not only significant because of its military merit and the role it played in defining Jackson's enduring legacy but also because it marked a very important transition for the valley's inhabitants. No longer would they experience war from reading newspapers or letters; they would witness war's dreadful hand personally as the campaign transformed the valley region from a homefront to a front line.

# Chapter 1

# "Employ the Invaders of the Valley"

By the first week of March 1862, anxieties had reached a fevered pitch in the heavily pro-Confederate community of Winchester, Virginia, as the inhabitants received news of an advancing Union army from Harpers Ferry—about 35,000 strong—under Major General Nathaniel P. Banks. "Quite a number of our people are leaving town," noted a resident of Winchester on March 3, "frightened almost to death of the Yankees, that they will come and catch them."[3] As many of Winchester's Confederate civilians evacuated the town, General Thomas J. "Stonewall" Jackson began preparations to secure the safety of his small Confederate force of about 3,500 troops. Jackson ordered his army's commissary and quartermaster stores moved south to Strasburg.[4] Jackson also took measures to secure the safety of his wife, Mary Anna, who had been with her husband in Winchester since December. On March 3, Jackson sent Mary Anna to Strasburg, where she could board a train that would carry her farther south. "Early in March, when he found that he would be compelled to retire from Winchester," Mary Anna recalled of her husband's decision, "although his heart was yearning… he thought it was no longer safe for me to remain, and I was sent to a place of safety."[5]

Four days after Jackson's wife departed Winchester, Banks's force moved to within four miles of Winchester's outskirts, where they encountered Confederate cavalry from Colonel Turner Ashby's command. After a small skirmish, Banks withdrew his army toward Bunker Hill. While Ashby's troopers pushed Banks north, Jackson placed his army in defensive

General Thomas J. "Stonewall" Jackson. *Courtesy of the Winchester-Frederick County Historical Society.*

positions several miles north of Winchester and dared Banks to attack. Banks refused to accept Jackson's invitation. "I was in hopes that they would advance on me during the evening," Jackson wrote to his wife, "as I felt that God would give us the victory."[6] Ashby's audacity on the seventh, as well as Jackson's willingness to offer Banks battle, "impressed" the Union commander "with the conviction that the Confederate force was much greater than it was in reality."[7]

Despite the "excellent spirits" of Jackson's army following Banks's advance on March 7, Winchester's Confederate civilians feared the imminence of Federal occupation.[8] "The people are all crazy—perfectly frantic for fear this place will be evacuated and the Yanks nab them," penned Winchester's Kate Sperry on March 7.[9] As tensions mounted over the next several days, Banks received information from a Unionist sympathizer in Winchester that

Jackson would withdraw from Winchester. Additional reports confirmed that Jackson had a considerably smaller force than Banks.[10] Confidently, Banks sent word to Washington, D.C., on March 8: "Our troops are in good health and spirits, eager for work…Our troops are…pressing forward in the direction of Winchester."[11]

The same day that Banks informed his superiors that his men pressed "forward in the direction of Winchester," Jackson wrote to his superior, General Joseph E. Johnston, that he greatly desired "to hold" Winchester.[12] Additionally, Jackson implored Johnston for reinforcements. "The very idea of re-enforcements coming to Winchester would, I think," Jackson informed his chief, "be a damper to the enemy, in addition to the fine effect that would be produced on our own troops."[13] The strategic situation, however, precluded Johnston from granting Jackson's request. Johnston, whose army was in the process of withdrawing from Manassas Junction to Richmond's defense, could ill-afford to offer any additional support to Jackson.[14] While Johnston

General Joseph E. Johnston. *Courtesy of the Winchester-Frederick County Historical Society.*

did not necessarily want Jackson to evacuate Winchester, Johnston believed that it was more important for Jackson to keep his army intact so that it could serve as a distraction to General George B. McClellan's operation against Richmond. Johnston hoped that once Jackson withdrew from Winchester, he could "employ the invaders of the Valley, but without exposing himself to the danger of defeat, by keeping so near the enemy as to prevent him from making any considerable detachment to reinforce McClellan."[15]

As it became more evident that Jackson would have to withdraw, he decided to arrest scores of area Unionists to protect his operational security. By some estimates, about 10 percent of Winchester's population held Unionist sympathies. The reasons for these sympathies varied—some were transplanted Northerners, others disagreed with secession and slavery and a portion belonged to religious groups such as Quakers and Mennonites, who refused to side with the Confederacy.[16] After a declaration of martial law on March 10, Jackson seized scores of male Unionists who lived in Winchester and the immediate surrounding area.[17] Among the Unionists seized by Jackson was Winchester's Charles Chase. Confederate soldiers entered the aged and infirm Chase's home and ripped him from his sofa. "To take an old man lying sick on the sofa is outrageous," recalled Chase's daughter Julia.[18]

As Julia learned of the arrests of other Unionists, she could only write, "We are fallen upon fearful times, great many Union people have been put in the guard house."[19] Another area resident recalled that Jackson's arrest of Unionist sympathizers "was the most humiliating sight…since the opening of the war. Gray-haired and prominent citizens marched like felons through the streets, tramping through mud and rain between files of soldiers."[20]

Despite the measures that Jackson took to secure his army for a withdrawal, Jackson maintained some degree of hope that his subordinates would support him in his desire to not relinquish Winchester without a fight. On the evening of March 11, Jackson dined at the home of Reverend Robert Graham on Braddock Street. When Jackson arrived for dinner, Reverend Graham recalled that Jackson was "all aglow with pleasant excitement because of the splendid behaviour of the troops, and their eagerness to meet the enemy."[21] Following dinner, Jackson left Graham's and proposed a surprise attack on the enemy that night. His subordinates disapproved and instead urged Jackson to withdraw. Prudence intervened and Jackson agreed to pull out.[22] Although Jackson opted to heed the advice of his brigade commanders, he "was bitterly distressed and mortified," noted Reverend

Graham, "at the necessity of leaving the people he loved dearly."[23] Amid his disappointment that evening, Jackson learned a valuable lesson from the experience of his war council: to never hold one nor ask for his subordinates' opinions again. An officer from Jackson's command noted that his council of war in Winchester was "the first and last time…that he ever summoned a council of war."[24]

Once Winchester's Confederate citizenry received confirmation of Jackson's withdrawal, they took measures to secure their property and prepare for what would become the first of many Union occupations. "From twelve till after one, we were very busy," recorded the staunch Confederate Mary Greenhow Lee, "putting in place of safety silver, papers, sword, flags, with my clothes, war letters, &c."[25] Other Confederate civilians in Winchester secured not only personal possessions but also bade farewell to loved ones who served in Jackson's command. Cornelia McDonald recalled that on the night of March 11 "there were hurried preparations and hasty farewells, and sorrowful faces turning away from those they loved best, and were leaving, perhaps forever."[26]

As Jackson's army marched south, Banks prepared to occupy Winchester. Banks approached cautiously and methodically. An artillerist in Banks's army stated that the army had to move "slow for fear of a fight."[27] The fortifications constructed by Jackson during the war's early months also presented an imposing sight to Banks's troops. "Several earthworks were observable, and we looked for a great battle," recalled General Alpheus Williams, one of Banks's division commanders. "It was an exciting sight."[28] Federal pickets inched their way toward the earthworks but found them vacant. While Banks's army occupied the earthworks, Winchester's mayor, John B.T. Reed, moved out to meet the Federal soldiers and surrender the town. With the town's surrender complete, the Federals marched into Winchester triumphantly.

Initially, the reception of the Union army by the citizens proved optimistic to Banks's troops. One of Banks's staff officers, David Hunter Strother, noted that as the Union army entered town, he "saw a group of men, women, and children waving handkerchiefs and welcoming us with every demonstration of delight." Interspersed throughout the crowd were area slaves and free blacks who looked upon Banks's men as potential agents of freedom.[29] Unionists and area African Americans reveled in the occupation. "Glorious news," confided Unionist Julia Chase to her journal on March 12.

General Nathaniel P. Banks. *Courtesy of the author.*

"The Union Army took possession of Winchester today and the glorious flag is waving over our town."[30]

While Unionists and African Americans applauded the sight of Union soldiers, the town's overwhelming Confederate majority loathed the spectacle before their eyes. Most citizens could not even bring themselves to come out of their homes to watch Banks's troops march into town. "The town during the entrance presented a sad and sullen appearance," noted John Peyton Clark. "Many of the houses of the citizens were entirely closed, few, perhaps none of the respectable portion of the town were conspicuous on the street."[31] Mary Greenhow Lee lamented, "All is over and we are prisoners in our own houses." Despite her melancholy tone, Mary Lee believed that it had been for the best, as she knew deep down inside that Jackson would not have been able to defeat Banks's army. "I remembered how thankful I was,"

Lee reflected on the evening of March 12, "that Jackson had not risked a battle, and that our precious little army was safe."[32]

Winchester's Confederate citizens resented the presence of Banks's men and did all they could to exhibit their disdain. Chief among those who did all they could to show their resentment were the town's Confederate women. When Union officers began to post the Stars and Stripes atop some of the town's buildings, the Confederate women took great pains to not walk in the flag's shadow. "None of the girls in the neighborhood will walk under it," Kate Sperry recalled. "They go out in the mud round it and on the pavement again." Union soldiers who watched these antics became outraged. "It makes them furious, the horrid cutthroats," Sperry noted. "I'm sure they'll stretch one across the whole street."[33] Other Confederate women cursed at Union soldiers, and some even created stories to frighten their occupiers. The 2nd Massachusetts' Lieutenant Robert Gould Shaw encountered one

Mary Greenhow Lee was arguably one of Winchester's staunchest Confederate civilians. Her hatred for anything Union led to her exile from Winchester in February 1865 by Union general Philip H. Sheridan. *Courtesy of the Winchester-Frederick County Historical Society.*

citizen who informed him that after the First Battle of Bull Run, some of Winchester's Confederate sympathizers collected and sold "Northern skulls" for ten dollars. After experiencing the venomous nature of the town's Confederate women, Shaw did not know what think. "I don't know whether to believe these things or not," Shaw wrote two days after Banks's army occupied Winchester.[34] When the chaplain of the 2nd Massachusetts heard these reports, he was not surprised. "But I am not at all surprised," noted Chaplain Alonzo Quint. "I have ceased to feel any wonder at the brutalities of the slaveholding people."[35]

Regardless of the tales that the Confederate civilians told Banks's men, Union soldiers did all they could during the first several days of their occupation to root out secessionist sentiment. Banks's troops searched homes for Confederate symbols or stockpiles of supplies being kept for Confederate soldiers. For example, on March 14, Union soldiers searched the home of John Peyton Clark, as they had received reports that his family was hiding a Confederate flag.[36]

Additionally, some Union soldiers stole from local businesses. "The meanness of these wretches is inconceivable and scarcely comprehensible to one who has not associated all his life with highway robbers and pick-pockets," Clark confided to his journal. "They do not hesitate to go into a store under the pretence of buying a penny's worth and steal anything they can lay their hands on."[37]

Despite the rowdy behavior of some of Banks's command, what undoubtedly proved most galling to the area's Confederate sympathizers was Banks's policy toward slaves. Banks, an abolitionist, did all that he could during his time in the valley to break slavery by encouraging slaves to run away.[38] "They are beginning to carry off numbers of servants," noted Laura Lee on March 14, "some to the camps, and some to work on the railroad at Harper's Ferry."[39] Kate Sperry simply observed three days later that the slaves "are running off continually."[40] In addition to encouraging slaves to leave their masters, Banks's men punished any white inhabitant of Winchester who mistreated a slave. Just three days after Banks's army entered Winchester, John Peyton Clark witnessed Union soldiers arrest one of his neighbors for hitting a female servant.[41]

As Banks's men occupied Winchester, the Lincoln administration assessed Union war strategy and McClellan's ability as general in chief. On the date that Jackson determined to evacuate Winchester, Lincoln summoned his cabinet to discuss McClellan's future. The previous day, McClellan had marched his army toward Johnston's Confederate positions near Manassas. When the Union commander arrived there, he found that Johnston had abandoned Manassas. McClellan then informed Lincoln that he would pursue Johnston, but he did not. Additionally, when Northern newspaper reporters investigated the vacant Confederate positions, they discovered that they were weak and ill-equipped.[42]

Based on those reports and the belief that McClellan could not run an effective campaign with the Army of the Potomac while managing the responsibilities as general in chief, Lincoln stripped McClellan of his overall command and allowed him only to command the Army of the Potomac, which now prepared to strike Richmond from the Virginia Peninsula.[43] Lincoln also directed McClellan to make certain that ample forces remained behind to leave the capital "entirely secure."[44] Although McClellan did not necessarily like this directive, because it took troops away from his campaign against Richmond, it became a condition upon which Lincoln's support for the Peninsula Campaign rested.[45] Amid Lincoln's many decisions that March, he also issued an order that restructured the Army of the Potomac into five corps. As a result, Banks's corps in the valley now held the designation of V Corps.[46]

Banks's newly minted corps soon found its ranks reduced as part of Lincoln's instructions to provide for Washington, D.C.'s security. Shortly after Banks occupied Winchester, General John Sedgwick's division was ordered to Manassas to help protect the capital. By March 16, McClellan pushed for Banks to send the bulk of his remaining force out of the valley and leave behind only one brigade to guard and oversee the rebuilding of the Baltimore & Ohio Railroad.[47]

This order caused some consternation in General Banks. At the time, Banks did not know Stonewall Jackson's precise location, overall strength or intentions. Before he could carry out the missive, Banks ordered a reconnaissance toward Strasburg. This burden fell on the shoulders of General James Shields. An Irish immigrant, Shields had been one of Lincoln's early political obstacles in Illinois. Tensions between the two mounted so much that in 1842 Shields challenged Lincoln to a duel. With the outbreak of war, however, Lincoln needed Shields's support and offered him a general's commission. Shields, like Banks and many other commanders who fought in the valley in 1862, held their posts due to political clout rather than military ability.[48]

General James Shields. *Courtesy of the author.*

On March 18, Shields's command marched out of Winchester and headed south in the direction of Strasburg. As the Federal forces marched into the various communities along the Valley Pike, Confederate civilians wondered what Shields's troops intended. When his force marched into Middletown—scene of the 1864 Battle of Cedar Creek—area civilians held preconceived notions about the barbarity of Federal troops from stories that had trickled in from Winchester. Much to their surprise, however, they found that Shields's men held real "human" qualities. "At first we thought the Yankees were a set of scoundrels, and we were dreading 'em," noted a fourteen-year-old boy in Middletown. "We didn't know what they looked like until Banks raided through here. But when we got acquainted we found they were human with about the same faults and virtues as our own men."[49]

When Shields marched through Middletown—a place identified by one soldier as "a village of but few inhabitants"—he halted his men on the northern bank of Cedar Creek. Despite his desire to push south, Shields could not, as Colonel Turner Ashby's troopers fired the bridge.[50] That evening, a portion of Shields's command built an impromptu bridge and camped on the southern banks of Cedar Creek, while other elements of Shields's division camped on the farm of Solomon and Caroline Heater. As Shields's troops established their camp, several of his officers spoke with the Heaters and discovered that their two sons had served in the Confederate army. Immediately the unidentified group of officers wanted to arrest Solomon Heater. Promptly, General Shields intervened and told them to leave the Heater family alone. Although the Heaters' sons might have served in the Confederacy and Solomon favored secession, Caroline Heater held Unionist loyalties. Jacob Larrick, the proprietor of a hotel and tavern in Middletown, recalled the event: "Gen. Shields told them to let Mr. Heater alone, that his wife was a Union woman."[51]

By March 20, Shields had pulled his force back to Winchester. The reconnaissance placated the members of the Union high command and caused them to believe that Jackson's small force posed no major threat. Armed with this belief, Union troops were now diverted from the valley to either protect the capital or support McClellan's operations. The paring down of Union forces in the valley resumed on the same day as Shields's withdrawal to Winchester when General Williams's division received orders to march to Centreville.[52] Meanwhile, Shields's departure brought despair to Colonel Ashby. This "Knight of the Valley" believed that Shields's

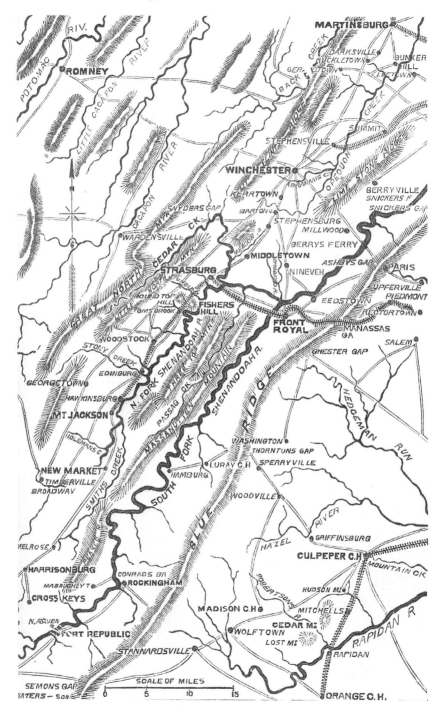

Area of operations in the Shenandoah Valley in 1862. *From* Pictorial History of the Great War, *1870.*

movement portended a much larger removal of Federal forces from the valley to support McClellan's operations. Ashby reported to Jackson that Banks's force was withdrawing from the valley with wagon trains carrying enough supplies to equip twelve thousand men.[53] When Jackson received this information, he became "apprehensive that the Federals would leave" the Shenandoah Valley.[54]

Two days before Ashby reported his intelligence to Jackson, Stonewall received a communiqué from General Johnston that directed the small force in the valley to do whatever necessary in order to prevent Banks's force from leaving the valley and reinforcing McClellan's operations against the Confederate capital. "It is important to keep that army in the valley," Johnston wrote Jackson, "& that it should not reinforce McClellan."[55] With that directive in mind, Jackson had no other alternative than to march his army north to strike the remaining Federals near Winchester and prevent them from leaving the valley. At that moment, Jackson's role in the valley had been established: to utilize the valley as a diversionary theater of war in order to protect Richmond and, in turn, the hopes of the Confederacy.

Chapter 2

# "Defeated, but not Routed nor Demoralized"

As a cold wind whipped through the Shenandoah Valley on the morning of March 22, 1862, Stonewall Jackson's small army of about 3,500 men marched north from their camps around Mount Jackson. Some soldiers in the Confederate column believed battle to be imminent and therefore turned their thoughts to God. Vices such as cards and tobacco were discarded, and some looked instead to their Bibles for comfort.[56] While some of Jackson's men lamented their futures, Jackson marched his column at a torrid pace. By day's end, Jackson's army had reached Strasburg, nearly thirty miles from their starting point that day. Some of Jackson's men found it difficult to maintain the march's rapid pace. John Casler, a veteran of the Stonewall Brigade, noted simply that "it was difficult to keep up with the troops."[57]

While Jackson's infantry hastened north, Confederate cavalry under Colonel Turner Ashby rode ahead of the army toward Winchester. On the southern outskirts of Newtown (present-day Stephens City), a young boy from Winchester greeted Ashby's troops and informed them that all of the Union forces had evacuated Winchester. "Between Middletown and Newtown we met a boy from Winchester," recalled a member of Ashby's command, "who told us that the Yanks all left town this morning."[58] By the time Ashby's command arrived in the vicinity of Kernstown, they realized that not all of Union troops had departed the valley—they spied Union pickets from the 1st Michigan Cavalry watering their horses in Hoge Run.[59] After they saw Ashby, the Michiganders mounted quickly and dashed toward Winchester. Ashby followed close on their heels. When Colonel Thornton F.

Colonel Turner Ashby. *From* Battles and Leaders of the Civil War.

Colonel Thornton Brodhead.
*Courtesy of the author.*

Brodhead—the Union cavalry chief in the valley that March—learned of Ashby's presence, he ordered Lieutenant Colonel Joseph T. Copeland's 1st Michigan Cavalry and Major Benjamin Chamberlain's 1st Virginia (U.S.) Cavalry to take positions on Winchester's southern outskirts astride the Valley Pike near Abraham Hollingsworth's gristmill.[60] While Copeland and Chamberlain positioned their commands, Ashby rolled three cannons from Captain R. Preston Chew's Battery into position several hundred yards from the Union line, which "kept up a brisk fire."[61]

Soon, additional cavalry, artillery and infantry support arrived near Hollingsworth's Mill. Unfortunately, as Shields directed the placement of guns from Captain James F. Huntington's Battery H, 1st Ohio Artillery, a shell fragment from one of Chew's guns fractured Shields's left arm above the elbow. Additionally, Shields suffered a bruised shoulder and injured his left side.[62] According to one account written several days after the skirmish, Shields shrugged off the wound. His adjutant general, Major Harry Armstrong, reportedly went to Shields and informed his commander that he was wounded in the arm. Armstrong remembered that "the gallant Shields told him 'Yes…but say nothing about it.'" The staff officer then reported that Shields "gave a fresh order to the artillery, and continued on the field till he satisfied himself that all was right."[63] Other accounts present Shields's wounding in less heroic terms. A Union surgeon who tended Shields on the field stated that the general fainted after being helped back onto his horse. After Shields passed out, the Union surgeon—Dr. H.M. McAbee—placed Shields into a carriage that, unfortunately for Shields, became a target for Confederate gunners.[64] Captain Chew ordered his men to "[g]ive that carriage a shot, it may be carrying some important game." Obediently, the artillerists unleashed their fire. "We turned one gun on it," remembered gunner George Neese, "and our shell exploded near the vehicle, and it soon after disappeared from the field."[65]

Confidence among Ashby's men soared. Ashby sensed weakness and ordered several companies to charge the Union position. The order proved ill-advised. "But in war things are not as they seem," remembered one soldier in Ashby's command. "Just before they got to the edge of town a regiment… rose from behind a fence and fired a volley at them at close range."[66] Luckily for Ashby's troopers, the Union soldiers aimed hastily and missed many of their targets. Still, the volley struck fear into the troopers and they withdrew. Shortly after the volley, Huntington's Ohio Battery opened on Ashby's men.

Union artillery chief Lieutenant Colonel Philip Daum wrote simply that when the Ohioans "opened fire upon the enemy," Ashby's command "immediately retreated."[67] A Confederate observed that Huntington's cannon "rendered our situation untenable, consequently we left forthwith and immediately."[68]

The sound of small arms and artillery fire on the twenty-second piqued the curiosity of area civilians. Confederate sympathizers particularly reveled at the prospect of a successful Confederate assault. "The citizens of Winchester," penned a soldier in the 29th Ohio, "were in high glee at the prospect of being rid of those odious Lincoln hirelings."[69] Some area civilians felt so assured of Confederate success that they prepared feasts for the Confederate soldiers. "Some were so sanguine of success to the Southern arms," recalled one Union infantryman, "that they prepared elegant repasts for the victors."[70] Unfortunately for the area's Confederate sympathizers, Ashby could not break through the Union line.

Despite Ashby's inability to fracture the Union defense, the small fight did give him the opportunity to communicate with several area civilians who informed him that the Federal army was in preparation for a complete withdrawal from Winchester.[71] Visual evidence also seemed to indicate to Ashby the presence of a small Union force. One of Ashby's men noted that during the skirmish they saw only "a few tents…apparently the town seemed to be evacuated by the enemy."[72] General Shields, in his after-action report (written one week after the skirmish on March 22), claimed that he purposely took measures to conceal his division to keep the Confederates "deceived as to our strength."[73] Ashby reportedly sent several scouts into Winchester, who confirmed the claims of a Union withdrawal and a small force.[74]

Once Ashby fell back, he reported the intelligence about the Union strength and withdrawal in Winchester to Jackson. With the directive from Johnston "to keep that Army in the Valley," Jackson knew that he needed to strike the Union force that, he believed, was numerically inferior to his own small command and prevent it from supporting McClellan's operations. Regardless of the military necessity to attack, Jackson grappled with a personal issue in determining whether to launch his offensive. If Jackson struck on March 23, it meant that he would have to fight on a Sunday. The intensely religious Jackson penned his wife Mary Anna that he "was greatly concerned" by this decision to order his men into battle on the Sabbath.[75] However, military prudence took over as "important considerations… rendered it necessary to attack."[76]

While Jackson determined to strike the Federals near Winchester, the Union command structure changed. With Shields wounded, the duties of field command fell on Colonel Nathan Kimball. A physician prior to the war, as well as a veteran of the Mexican-American War, Kimball held a reputation, according to an Ohio officer, as a "stout old fighter."[77] Although Kimball commanded troops on the field, General Shields still attempted to direct troop movements from his convalescent bed at the Seevers' house in Winchester. During the night of March 22, Shields ordered Kimball to take his original brigade and artillery from Lieutenant Colonel Daum's command to Kernstown. Colonel Jeremiah Sullivan's brigade positioned itself behind Kimball's command to guard against an assault by way of Cedar Creek Grade, the Front Royal Road, Berryville Pike or Romney Road. Colonel Erastus Tyler's brigade, along with the Federal cavalry, remained in reserve that night.[78] As Shields tried to rest that evening, he felt confident that "all approaches by which the enemy could penetrate to this place were efficiently guarded."[79]

Colonel Nathan Kimball.
*From* Battles and Leaders of the Civil War.

On the morning of March 23, both General Shields and General Banks conferred about the likelihood of a major attack from Jackson's force. Both men agreed that "Jackson could not be tempted to hazard himself" to strike the Federal force. About 9:00 a.m., Banks, confident that Jackson posed no immediate danger, decided to leave the valley for Washington, D.C.[80]

Interestingly, at about the same moment as Shields and Banks concluded that Jackson would not attack, Colonel Ashby appeared at Kimball's front. Ashby's cavalry, along with Captain Chew's three guns and four infantry companies under Captain John Q.A. Nadenbousch, deployed on the east side of the Valley Pike.[81] Chew's guns unlimbered and, at about 9:00 a.m., fired the first shots of the First Battle of Kernstown.[82] Kimball reacted swiftly. Colonel Samuel Carroll's 8th Ohio moved forward astride the Valley Pike, along with two companies of the 67th Ohio, to dislodge the Confederates. While the Ohioans occupied Ashby's attention, Kimball massed sixteen cannons from Lieutenant Colonel Daum's command atop Pritchard's Hill—a commanding eminence on the west side of the Valley Pike.

Chew's gunners targeted the cannons atop Pritchard's Hill. Confederate gunners lobbed shells into the Union position for about an hour, but with limited effect. The 5th Ohio's Lieutenant George Whitcamp—whose regiment stood in support of Daum's artillery—noted: "The fire from the enemy was heavy and constant, principally shell and round shot, which continued for about an hour…most of [Chew's] volleys went too far, which was very fortunate for our forces."[83]

Unfortunately for the Confederates, Daum's gunners fired with tremendous accuracy. "The Federal artillery was in position on a range of hills northwest of the town," recalled one of Chew's men, "and replied to our opening shots with a vim which at once bespoke that they meant business."[84] What further complicated the situation for Chew's artillery was the presence of a company of Andrew's Sharpshooters. The marksmen from Massachusetts, armed with heavy-barreled long-range target rifles, targeted the horses and gunners of Chew's command.[85] Within two hours after the Confederates fired the first shot, Ashby had no other alternative than to pull his command off the field. "When the sharpshooters opened on us with their long-range rifles, and the…artillery commenced firing on us," recalled a member of Ashby's command, "we abandoned our position and retreated under fire."[86]

Despite the moment's deadliness, some of Ashby's men—as was also the case among Union soldiers—seemed amazed at the sights and sounds of

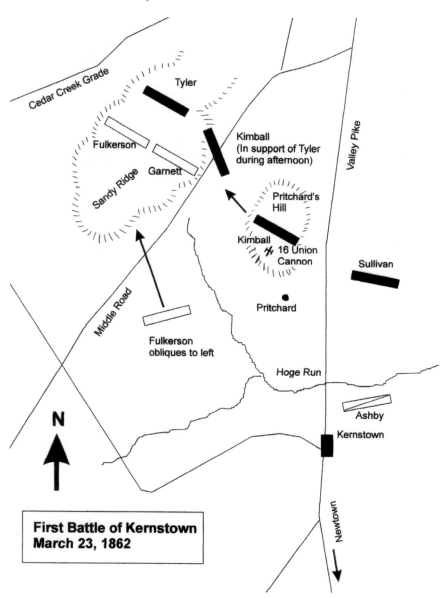

Map of First Battle of Kernstown. *Courtesy of the author.*

battle. For soldiers on both sides, the First Battle of Kernstown was their first major action, and some acted foolishly. During the initial part of the artillery bombardment, one of Chew's gunners, George Neese, stood in awe as he watched an artillery shell flying through the air toward his position. "I was so interested in the sky ball, in its harmless appearance, and surprised that a shell could be so plainly seen during its flight," Neese explained, "that I for a moment forgot that danger lurked in the black speck." When the percussion shell hit the ground, it brought Neese back to reality, as it "exploded and scattered itself in every direction around me, and threw up dirt and gravel like a volcano."[87]

Once Ashby left the field, a lull of about two hours ensued. Kimball assessed the situation and determined it best to remain in a defensive position. When Shields discovered Kimball's intentions to stay on the defensive, he advised Kimball to go on the offensive. Shields wanted Kimball to attack, as he believed, from his bed in Winchester, that the Confederate force in Kimball's front "was not strong enough."[88] The directive infuriated Kimball, and he refused to obey. "Convinced that the general did not comprehend the situation…and satisfied from his bed in the city five miles to the rear," Kimball explained, "he could not properly conduct the movements which might be required by the exigencies of the situation, I determined to remain on the defensive."[89]

While Kimball strengthened his defensive line, Stonewall Jackson moved the main body of his army toward the battlefield. At about 2:00 p.m., Jackson's force massed in Barton's Woods—located south of Kimball's lines on the west side of the Valley Pike. Initially, Jackson decided that he would wait until the following morning to strike Kimball's defenses.[90] As Jackson surveyed the Union line, particularly the sixteen Union cannons atop Pritchard's Hill, he reconsidered. The longer Jackson delayed an assault, the more time the Federals had to strengthen their position. "I deemed it best not to attack until morning," Jackson explained about two weeks after the battle, "but subsequently ascertaining that the Federals had a position from which our forces could be seen, I concluded that it would be dangerous to postpone it until the next day, as re-enforcements might be brought up during the night."[91]

After Jackson determined to attack Kimball's line, he next needed to figure out where to strike. A frontal assault against the Union artillery atop Pritchard's Hill held no chance for success, and an attack against the well-protected Union left flank also presented problems, as Ashby's command had discovered earlier in the day. Jackson knew that he needed to flank the right of Kimball's line.[92]

Jackson initially determined to turn Kimball's right with infantry. He sent Colonel Samuel Fulkerson's brigade of two regiments—the 23rd and 37th Virginia Infantry—through Barton's Woods and into an open field to strike the Union flank. Unfortunately for Fulkerson's men, Daum's artillery atop Pritchard's Hill saw every move. With the 37th Virginia in front, Fulkerson placed his brigade in column of divisions. As soon as they entered into an open field, Union artillery shelled Fulkerson's regiments. Fulkerson's advance slowed when his men had to stop to tear down a wooden plank fence and then encountered a marshy area. Fulkerson wrote simply that Daum's gunners "instantly opened a galling fire upon us…The ground at this point being marshy and several fences interposing, the advance was a good deal retarded but steady, the enemy all the while throwing shell and shot into the column with great rapidity."[93]

With Fulkerson under heavy fire, Jackson ordered General Richard B. Garnett—commander of the Stonewall Brigade—to move forward and support Fulkerson. However, General Garnett did not feel comfortable with the directive, as he had no idea of Fulkerson's mission.[94] Garnett obeyed Jackson's order, but he only supported Fulkerson with one of his regiments— Colonel Arthur Cummings's 33rd Virginia Infantry. Cummings's regiment met the same severe artillery fire as did Fulkerson's brigade. Cummings stated simply that his regiment was "under a heavy fire from the enemy's battery."[95] As artillery shells rained on the three Confederate regiments, Fulkerson and Garnett determined that no infantry assault could succeed. Both commanders decided to move their regiments farther to the west, to the base of Sandy Ridge—a commanding piece of high ground on Kimball's right flank that towered above Pritchard's Hill.[96]

The problems that confronted Jackson's infantry made Stonewall aware that infantry alone could not break Pritchard's Hill. Jackson now determined to position artillery atop Sandy Ridge to the west and blast the Federal flank. In order to execute the maneuver, however, Jackson needed to create a diversion against the Union left flank to allow the guns enough time to get into position. For this task, Jackson turned to the daring Colonel Ashby.[97] The Confederate cavalier, who fought with "marvelous audacity" during this point in the battle, distracted the Federals long enough for the deployment of Confederate cannon to Sandy Ridge.[98]

Between about 3:00 and 4:00 p.m., three Confederate batteries positioned themselves on Sandy Ridge and "commenced playing on the enemy."[99] "About 4 o'clock…Jackson…planted his batteries in commanding position," recalled Kimball, "and opened a heavy and well directed fire upon our batteries and their supports."[100]

As Confederate shells poured into the Union line atop Pritchard's Hill, Kimball realized that he needed to silence Jackson's guns or suffer total annihilation.

To quiet the Confederates on Sandy Ridge, Kimball turned to his reserve brigade, commanded by Colonel Erastus B. Tyler. During the battle's morning phase, Tyler's brigade of about 2,300 men was positioned in camps north of Winchester, but the soldiers could hear the distant small arms and artillery fire. As the battle intensified, Tyler's brigade marched from its camp to the area where the Cedar Creek Grade intersected the Valley Pike. Soldiers from Tyler's command noted that as they marched closer to the battlefield they encountered many curious Confederate civilians. "As we passed through Winchester to the south," recalled an officer in the 7th Ohio Infantry, "we emerged into an open plain. This was crowded with people, as were also the house-tops. They had assembled, apparently, for the purpose of seeing the Union army defeated and crushed, and to welcome the victors into the city."[101]

After Tyler received Kimball's order to move to Sandy Ridge, he marched his brigade west for about one mile along Cedar Creek Grade and then turned his column south to strike at the Confederates who had established position on Sandy Ridge in an area known as Rose Hill—the farm of Colonel William Glass of the 51st Virginia Militia. While Tyler positioned his men, Captain Lucius Robinson's Battery L, 1st Ohio Light Artillery, tried to distract the Confederate batteries. Within a minute after positioning themselves on ground northwest of Pritchard's Hill, and within about six hundred yards of Jackson's guns, Robinson's Battery began to take casualties. One member of the battery, John Brown, had his head completely shot off. Andrew Sharp, another member of Robinson's Battery, who was covered in Brown's blood and brains, became so disturbed by the horrific episode that he abandoned his post. One member of the battery stated simply, "Andrew Sharp, who threw his hands up to his face and seeing the blood thought himself mortally wounded, lit out, and we never saw him again."[102]

Meanwhile, Tyler's men marched toward the Confederate position. With the 7th Ohio in the lead, Tyler's men deployed against the Confederate position. Before Tyler's troops could see anything, musket fire from the 21st and 27th Virginia Infantry, who were posted behind a stone wall that traversed Sandy Ridge, greeted the Union brigade. As Tyler's line moved forward, a soldier in the 1st Virginia (U.S.) recalled, "No doubt every man thought at this time, while an almost unseen enemy was shooting at him, that absence

Colonel Joseph Thoburn.
*Courtesy of the Nicholas P.
Picerno Collection.*

of body was better than presence of mind...the enemy was doing his best to kill; the buzz and whistle of the balls, with now and then a pit or thugh as one hit the solid part of a man, was not pleasant music."[103] In addition to the fire from the two Virginia regiments, Confederate artillery also started to break up Tyler's command. "The grape and canister was tearing the bark from the trees over our heads," recalled a veteran of the 7th Ohio, "while the solid shot and shell made great gaps in their trunks...around and about us the air was thick with flying missiles."[104]

Under terrific fire, Colonel Tyler ordered Colonel Joseph Thoburn's 1st Virginia (U.S.) to capture an unoccupied portion of the stone wall to the left of the two Virginia regiments and flank the Confederate line.[105] As Thoburn's command moved toward the wall, Colonel Fulkerson moved his

Confederate brigade to occupy the same position. Both sides caught sight of each other, anticipated each other's intentions and dashed for the wall. "Both regiments charged for the fence about the same time," recalled a Confederate soldier, "and it was 'nip and tuck' which would reach it first."[106] Fulkerson's 37th Virginia reached the wall first and "opened a very destructive fire," noted Fulkerson, "which in a short time strewed the field with the dead and wounded of the enemy."[107] Sandie Pendleton, one of Jackson's staff officers, noted of the race for the wall: "There was an exciting race for this [wall] and the 37th Regiment got to it first, pouring a volley into the enemy."[108] Despite the inability of Thoburn's troops to reach the wall, some took cover behind a wall that joined and ran perpendicular to the Confederate position. The two enemies now fired at point-blank range.[109] Some Federal soldiers stated that at points during this phase of the battle the lines of the opposing armies stood as close as five yards apart.[110]

Tyler's brigade soon confronted additional enemy fire from troops from Garnett's command, which extended the Confederate right along the stone wall. The intensity of the fire compelled each soldier in Tyler's brigade to fire as rapidly as possible. "The roar of musketry soon became continuous," remembered one of Thoburn's veterans. "All ideas of platoon firing were

Union veterans who fought in the Shenandoah Valley in 1864 gather for a photograph in front of the famed stone wall at Kernstown in the mid-1880s after touring the battlefield at Rose Hill. *Courtesy of the United States Army Military History Institute.*

forgotten, it was simply fire at will."[111] "The roar of musketry was deafening," noted another veteran of Tyler's command. "The only evidence of life on that gory field, was the vomiting forth of flame and smoke from thousands of well-aimed muskets."[112] Bullets riddled everything that stood in their path. Regimental standards were torn to pieces. The regimental flag of the 7th Ohio was struck by twenty-eight bullets and the staff cut in half.[113] In the battle's aftermath, a Wisconsin soldier who walked over the ground noted that "scarcely a bush or a tree but showed the marks of bullets at a height of three to six feet from the ground."[114] To soldiers not involved in the fight on Rose Hill, the sound of the musketry seemed appalling. A gunner in Chew's Battery—posted on the opposite end of the Confederate line—turned to one of his comrades and exclaimed, "My God, just listen to the musketry! There will be no more fighting these armies after to-day, for they will all be killed on both sides this evening."[115]

After about an hour of intense firing, Tyler needed support or would have to quit the field. Kimball reacted promptly and redeployed regiments from the area of Pritchard's Hill to Sandy Ridge.[116] The Confederate defenders now

An idealized portrayal of Colonel Erastus Tyler's attack at Kernstown. *Courtesy of the author.*

fought with a sense of desperation. As reinforcements from Ohio attacked Garnett's brigade, the color-bearer of the 5th Virginia Infantry reportedly jumped over the stone wall, waved the regiment's flag and dared the Union soldiers to attack. Union Lieutenant C.W. Fahrion, who reportedly witnessed this episode, noted: "So astonishing was this exhibition of nerve that my men ceased firing and sang out, 'Don't shoot that man, he is too brave to die.'" The Confederate color-bearer then saluted the attacking Union soldiers and returned to his side of the wall.[117]

Confusion also dominated this phase of the battle. Troops from the 5th Ohio accused the 14th Indiana of firing into their backs. As the 84th Pennsylvania struck the Confederate line, the Confederate defenders attempted to confuse the Pennsylvanians by yelling out to stop firing as they, too, were guilty of shooting into the backs of Union regiments. Although this caused the 84th to cease its fire for a moment, the Union attack soon resumed. The regiment's commander, Colonel William Murray, urged his men to continue to press the enemy. Unfortunately, as Murray encouraged his regiment, a Confederate bullet struck him in the head and killed him instantly.[118] After the battle, Colonel Kimball lamented, "Colonel Murray… fell while bravely leading forward his gallant men, amidst a perfect storm of shot and shell."[119]

Despite the intense Confederate fire and mounting casualties, the Union line continued to press forward. As the sun began to set, the Confederate line—with no additional support—began to show signs of decay. With ammunition running low and darkness descending over the battlefield, General Garnett—the senior commander on this portion of the field—had received no additional directives from Jackson and ordered a withdrawal.[120] When Jackson encountered Confederate soldiers streaming to the rear, he became irate. When Jackson met a soldier from the 21st Virginia Infantry, he asked him where he was going. The Confederate soldier informed Jackson he had run out of ammunition. In style typical of Stonewall Jackson, the army commander told the private to "go back and give them the bayonet."[121] Immediately, Jackson considered how he might be able to reform his small army. Jackson grabbed Hugh Barr—a twenty-two-year-old drummer from the 5th Virginia—and ordered him to "beat the rally."[122]

Early accounts of the battle improperly portrayed Barr as a young child whom Jackson relied on to rally the army. Perhaps the potential romanticism of the moment prompted some early authors to deny Barr's age at the

An inaccurate, romanticized portrayal of Jackson's order to Confederate drummer Hugh Barr to "beat the rally." *From* The Life of Thomas J. Jackson: In Easy Words for the Young, *1899.*

time of the battle. Among those who depicted the event incorrectly was children's author and valley resident Mary Lynn Williamson, who in 1899 published *The Life of Thomas J. Jackson: In Easy Words for the Young.* "Seeing a drummer boy retreating like the rest," Williamson wrote, "he [Jackson] seized him by the shoulder, dragged him in full view of the soldiers, and said in the sternest tone, 'Beat the rally!'" Williamson's portrayal of the event, undoubtedly meant to inspire a generation of Southern children after the Civil War, included an illustration of the event that showed a young drummer boy rather than an adult being grabbed by Jackson to help reform the Confederate lines.[123]

Regardless of Jackson's efforts to rally his army, the Confederate line could not be reformed. With the Confederate defense cracked, Colonel Thornton Brodhead's Union cavalry now moved in to put the finishing touches on Jackson's army. When Lieutenant Colonel Joseph Copeland ordered the troopers of the 1st Michigan Cavalry to charge into the retreating Confederates, the men greeted it "with enthusiasm and executed with alacrity."[124] Although the Union cavalrymen reveled in the order to charge the enemy, they did confront obstacles that slowed their pursuit—namely, the number of fences that crossed the landscape. "The stone fences were great hindrances to our charge on the enemy," noted an Ohio cavalryman.[125]

At various points during the Confederate retreat, portions of Jackson's command attempted to stall the Union pursuit, but to no avail. Jackson pulled his army back to the vicinity of Newtown, several miles south of Kernstown. That night, Confederate soldiers collapsed with exhaustion. "We all scattered back as far as Newtown that night…and lay along the road," noted a Stonewall Brigade veteran, "every fellow for himself, building fires out of fence rails, and making ourselves as comfortable as we could after the fatigues of the day."[126] Despite their fatigue, spirits among Jackson's soldiers seemed somewhat optimistic in the battle's immediate aftermath. A Confederate artillerist noted of the army's morale: "Jackson gave up the field, repulsed, but not vanquished, defeated, but not routed nor demoralized."[127] Stonewall Jackson, too, believed that the battle had done little to diminish his army's spirits. Four days after the battle, Jackson wrote to his wife Mary Anna: "My little army is in excellent spirits. It feels that it inflicted a severe blow upon the enemy."[128]

By day's end, Kimball's force suffered about six hundred casualties, while Jackson's command suffered more than seven hundred casualties.[129] Surgeon William King, the medical director of the Union force in the valley, took immediate steps to secure the wounded. Campfires lit up the nighttime sky as parties of Union soldiers combed the field for wounded, who were then loaded into ambulances and sent to makeshift hospitals in Winchester.[130] "The ambulances have been running all day to the battle-field bringing in the wounded…presenting every variety of wound, some of them shocking and distressing to the last degree," noted Winchester's John Peyton Clark on March 24.[131] For the wounded who could not be moved, civilians in the Kernstown area assumed the daunting responsibility of caring for them. Samuel and Helen Pritchard—whose home sat at the base of the hill that bore their name and that became Jackson's initial tactical focus—transformed their three-story brick home into a safe haven for wounded soldiers.

After the battle, Randolph Martin, a resident of Kernstown, went to the Pritchard Farm and noted: "I was up on the battlefield which was on the Pritchard place the morning after the battle. The Yankee soldiers and some of the citizens were moving the wounded…some of which was taken over to Mr. Pritchard's house and a hospital was made of his house."[132] Apparently, Pritchard had been in a surly mood after the battle and muttered under his breath "that he was disappointed in the fight that he was in the hopes that Jackson would kill and capture all the Yankees this side of the Potomac."[133] This comment later came back to haunt Pritchard when he filed a claim for nearly $5,700 with the Southern Claims Commission in 1875 for damage done to his property throughout the course of the entire Civil War. Pritchard's remark on March 24, 1862, convinced the government—despite the care that he gave to Union soldiers throughout the war and his wife's unquestioned Unionist sympathies—that his loyalties rested with the Confederacy and, therefore, that his family was not entitled to financial compensation.[134]

The Pritchard House was transformed from a peaceful abode into a makeshift hospital after Kernstown. *Courtesy of the author.*

In Winchester, the civilians—whether they sympathized with the Union or Confederacy—put aside their allegiances and did what they could to alleviate the suffering of dying soldiers. As the staunchly Confederate Cornelia McDonald went to the various buildings in town converted into hospitals to offer assistance, she noted that for the moment humanity replaced hatred. When she arrived at the Farmer's Bank, she encountered a group of women comforting wounded Union soldiers. "The ladies looked pityingly down at them," McDonald recalled, "and tried to help them, though they did wear blue coats, and none of their own were there to weep over or help them."[135]

Laura Lee recalled of the women's mercy toward Union soldiers the day after Kernstown: "The ladies were hurrying to the hospitals to feed the poor creatures, friends and enemies alike."[136] Soon, Winchester's civilians, namely women, received some support in their mission of mercy about one week after the battle when Dorthea Dix and a contingent of nurses arrived in Winchester to care for the wounded. "Miss Dix has come and brought a corps of nurses, & to my inexpressible relief," noted Winchester's Mary Lee. "I shall not have to go to the Hospital again, unless something unforeseen occurs."[137]

While area civilians and Union doctors cared for the wounded, burial parties began the grisly work of interment. For many of the Union soldiers tasked with burying the dead, the horrifying scene became too much. "The ghastly aspect of the field after the wounded were removed before the dead were interred, was appalling. Some with the faces off, some with their heads off," recalled an observer, "some torn into fragments and frightfully mangled by the round shot and shell, and others simply but quite effectually killed by bullet wounds."[138] The scene around the stone wall presented perhaps the most terrible spectacle on the entire battlefield. "About the stone wall the enemy was strewn almost on top of each other in heaps of dead," recalled a newspaper reporter.[139]

Union burial parties initially only concerned themselves with the Union dead. When this news reached some of Winchester's Confederate civilians, they were appalled. Philip Williams, along with several other civilians, pleaded with Union commanders to allow a contingent of civilians to go out to the battlefield and bury the Confederate dead. On March 25, the Federals granted permission to the civilian contingent. The civilians, who performed the duty "in a suitable manner," did all they could to identify the dead and the locations of the graves. News of this act reached Jackson's army within one week after the battle and met with appreciation.[140] "The people of Winchester went out and had our dead interred decently," noted Sandie Pendleton six days after the fight, "taking descriptions of each one not identified, and numbering the graves."[141]

As area civilians did what they could to alleviate the suffering of the wounded and bury the Confederate dead, their hopes for Confederate success in the valley diminished with Jackson's loss. Not only did the scenes of the dead and dying weaken their spirits, but so too did the sight of about two hundred Confederate prisoners of war being marched up Market Street on the way to train cars that would carry them to Union prison camps. As the column of Confederate prisoners passed through Winchester, the townspeople lined the streets and tried to give them food and other supplies. What made the scene even more heart-rending was that the civilians either were related to or at the very least knew many of the prisoners. "Among these were some of our dear friends," recalled John Peyton Clark. "The ladies held out baskets of biscuits and perhaps other things which they took as they moved along."[142]

Four days after the battle, Secretary of State William Seward and Secretary of War Edwin Stanton arrived in Winchester to congratulate the Union troops and tour the battlefield. The scene shocked the town's Confederate sympathizers. Kate Sperry recorded in her diary: "Old Seward and Stanton Sec of State and Sec. of War came this evening to visit us and the battlefield—the old 'rips'—to think our soil should ever be desecrated by the tread of such black hearted villains."[143] Certainly these members of Lincoln's cabinet felt the animosity. When they returned to Washington, D.C., Seward met with President Lincoln, who inquired as to the strength of Unionist sentiment in the Winchester area. Seward told Lincoln simply: "The men are all in the army, & the women are the devils."[144]

The Union victory at Kernstown elevated spirits in the North. Many regarded it as the first major success in Virginia—a theater of war that had not been that kind to Union operations thus far. "The people throughout the North hailed it with almost unbounded joy," recalled a veteran of the battle. "This victory was something tangible, and revived their spirits at once."[145] Some also saw it as a battle that diminished the image of Stonewall Jackson born at the First Battle of Bull Run. "The victory heartened up the North very greatly," noted a Union veteran, "and it threw a shadow upon the reputation which Stonewall Jackson had gained at Bull Run."[146] The idea that Union forces defeated Stonewall Jackson became something that Union veterans of Kernstown cherished for the remainder of their lives. In the war's aftermath, veterans of the battle created an organization known as the Winchester Club. Annually the veterans gathered on the battle's anniversary to commemorate their victory over Stonewall Jackson with "a jolly, good time [of]...hard tack, coffee, stories, and fun."[147]

Perhaps no one enjoyed the victory over Jackson more than General Shields. Despite his absence on the field during the battle, Shields claimed credit and embellished Jackson's numbers tremendously. In his initial communiqué about the Union victory, Shields placed Jackson's force at about fifteen thousand—twice the size of the Union force. Reports filed several days later estimated the Confederate force at a minimum of eleven thousand, still much larger than Shields's division.[148] Even some regimental historians continued to perpetrate the myth that Shields's division defeated a numerically superior force at Kernstown. The 29th Ohio's historian J. Hamp SeCheverell wrote that at Kernstown "Stonewall Jackson, the pride of the South and by many considered the bravest generals in the army, was whipped, and that, too, by a force much inferior in numbers."[149]

Although some regimental historians continued to promulgate the myth of a numerically larger Confederate army, one item that some veterans would not let persist was the idea that Shields deserved credit for the victory. A veteran from Tyler's brigade attempted to correct the record after the Civil War's end. "After the battle...General Shields showed a disposition to appropriate the laurels won by others to himself," recalled the regimental historian of the 7th Ohio. "Colonel Kimball was mainly instrumental in achieving the victory, assisted, of course, by those under his command. The skillful manner, however, in which the troops were managed, was entirely due to him."[150] Another veteran wrote that General Shields "sounded his own trumpet with skill and unflagging persistence, and appropriated the credit for all he, could lay his hands upon...The credit for the victory was really due to...Col. Kimball and the excellent Colonels."[151]

Despite the work of some regimental historians to correct the record and diminish Shields's undeserved legacy, a variety of popular efforts countered their labors. For instance, the art firm of Currier & Ives attempted to transform Shields into a legend by using the fight on March 22 as the setting for a lithograph. It depicted Shields astride his horse gallantly leading his men in the skirmish on March 22. Furthermore, in the early 1900s the Baltimore & Ohio Railroad published its guide, *The Blue and the Gray: Battlefields on or*

# "Defeated, but not Routed nor Demoralized"

This Currier and Ives print, portraying General Shields in more than heroic terms during the small skirmish on March 22, 1862, helped improperly elevate his status after the First Battle of Kernstown. *Courtesy of the Library of Congress.*

*Near the Baltimore and Ohio.* When the guide discussed Kernstown, it heaped all praise on Shields and made no mention of Kimball. "Four miles from Winchester is Kernstown," the guide informed its travelers, "where the battle was fought between Jackson and Shields, and where the gallant hero…defeated the redoubtable Stonewall and forced him from his position, compelling him to retreat from the Valley."[152]

In retrospect, Shields's embellishments, which fomented unearned praise, worked more in favor of Stonewall Jackson's interests than Shields's. When General Banks learned of Shields's report, he redirected General Williams's division back to the Shenandoah Valley, with additional troops to follow. In all, the War Department redirected about twenty thousand Union troops—who could have been utilized to support McClellan's operations on the Virginia Peninsula—to deal with Jackson.[153] "The battle of Kernstown," recalled a member of Jackson's command after the war, "if not to be claimed as a victory for the Confederates served all the purposes of one."[154]

While the battle's strategic consequences became clearer, Jackson still bemoaned his tactical loss at Kernstown and looked to placed blame. In Jackson's perspective, only one person could shoulder responsibility for the defeat: General Garnett. Since the beginning of the year, Jackson believed Garnett to be incapable of command and even vented his frustration with Garnett to the Confederate War Department.[155] At Kernstown, Jackson believed that Garnett performed poorly, from his support of Fulkerson to his withdrawal from Rose Hill. On April 1, Jackson ordered Sandie Pendleton to arrest Garnett. It came as a surprise to both Pendleton and Garnett. "I am…utterly amazed at it," Pendleton explained to his mother on April 3, "and knew nothing about it, until Genl. Jackson directed me to go arrest him, and relieve him from command 'for neglect of duty' on the 23d."[156] The veterans of the Stonewall Brigade reacted harshly to the news. "The

General Charles Winder. *From* Battles and Leaders.

brigade is in a very bad humor at [Garnett's arrest] for he was a pleasant man and exceedingly popular," Sandie Pendleton observed.[157] The brigade's regimental officers defended Garnett's conduct, but this meant nothing to Jackson. He had made up his mind. "The officers in the brigade thought General Garnett was right," recalled Henry Kyd Douglas, "in fact I do not know an exception to this opinion."[158]

What further enraged the men of the Stonewall Brigade was Jackson's decision to replace Garnett with General Charles S. Winder. The Stonewall Brigade veterans disliked the appointment of the Marylander to command and exhibited that displeasure to Winder. "General Winder was received in sulky and resentful silence," noted one of Jackson's staff officers. The men even gave Jackson the cold shoulder for nearly a month and refused to cheer him.[159] These actions from his former brigade—which in the eyes of one of Jackson's staff officers bordered on insubordination—did little to disconcert Jackson, who turned his attention to the reorganization and reinforcement of his command.[160] Jackson knew that it would only be a matter of time before a Federal force pursued his army, and he needed to make preparations to meet that threat.

# Chapter 3

# "GOD BLEST OUR ARMS"

Once Stonewall Jackson pulled his army back to the area of Rude's Hill—a defensive position several miles south of Mount Jackson—the commander of Confederate forces in the valley looked to strengthen his command. To achieve this objective, Jackson first looked to how he might utilize the valley's geography to divide and conquer. To aid him in his understanding of the valley's intricacies, Jackson turned to Jedediah Hotchkiss. Although Hotchkiss spent the first eighteen years of his life in the North, Hotchkiss possessed an intricate knowledge of the valley. At age eighteen, Hotchkiss and a friend came to the valley for a five-hundred-mile excursion. By the autumn of 1847, Hotchkiss moved to the valley and eventually became headmaster at the Loch Willow School in Churchville. From the moment he arrived in Augusta County, Virginia, until the outbreak of Civil War, Hotchkiss used his free time exploring the valley, while teaching himself cartography and surveying.[161] On March 26, three days after the tactical defeat at Kernstown, Jackson summoned Hotchkiss—who at the time served as an officer in the Augusta County Militia Battalion, sent to strengthen Jackson's army—to his headquarters. "I want you to make me a map of the Valley, from Harper's Ferry to Lexington," Jackson informed Hotchkiss, "showing all the points of offence and defence in those places."[162]

While Hotchkiss set out on his mapmaking mission, Jackson looked to increase the size of his army. For this task, Jackson received some support from both Virginia's governor and, eventually, the Confederate government. On March 28, 1862, Confederate president Jefferson Davis proposed conscription to replenish the Confederacy's ranks. Although an unpopular proposal, few believed that the Confederate Congress would block the necessary measure. Even though the Conscription Act did not take effect until April 16, Virginia's Governor John Letcher anticipated its approval and on March 29 disbanded the commonwealth's militia and ordered those companies to be absorbed into already-extant Confederate regiments.[163] Letcher's directive did not please all of Virginia's militiamen, as some preferred to make the decision themselves as to where they would serve. "But the militia did not like that way of doing business," noted a veteran of the Stonewall Brigade, "for they considered it certain death to be put into the Stonewall Brigade, and wanted to choose their own companies."[164] While some accepted their new assignments, others did not and simply chose to run away and organize their own companies for service in the Confederate army. "The consequence was the greater number of them ran off and went home to their respective counties," recalled a soldier in Jackson's army, "and there formed cavalry companies, organized new regiments, and did good service during the balance of the war."[165]

When a contingent of militiamen from Rockingham County received orders to report to Jackson's army, they simply refused and retreated to the Blue Ridge Mountains. To deal with this "Rockingham Rebellion," Jackson sent Lieutenant Colonel John R. Jones, a county native who knew the area well, to end the resistance and bring these men to justice. In the eyes of some of Jackson's men, these militia soldiers from Rockingham were guilty of desertion and deserved the direst punishment. Lieutenant Colonel Jones, along with four infantry companies, one cavalry company and two artillery pieces, found the disgruntled militiamen and shelled their position in the Blue Ridge. In a matter of moments, twenty-four of the militiamen surrendered (one had been killed). One elderly woman who lived near the militia hideout noted of the episode: "The deserters had mortified in the Blue Ridge, but that General Jackson sent a foot company and a critter company to ramshag the Blue Ridge and capture them."[166]

Another segment of the valley's population also resisted conscription into the Confederacy's service: Unionists. Among the valley's Unionist sympathizers who feared being forced into the Confederate army were religious denominations such as Quakers, Mennonites and Dunkards. Jackson understood that these individuals presented some problems to his efforts to increase his army's size. Fear prompted Unionist sympathizers to organize a

Unionist Underground Railroad in Rockingham County. In an operational manner similar to the Underground Railroad that aided slaves, the Unionist Underground secreted males subject to Confederate conscription and spirited them to Keyser, Virginia (now West Virginia), a depot along the Baltimore & Ohio Railroad.[167] An untold number of Unionists escaped conscription in the spring of 1862; however, not all could. Those who could not flee attempted to desert Jackson's ranks once enlisted or, at the very minimum, refused to shoot in combat. "There are three religious denominations in this military district which are opposed to the war. Eighteen [men] were recently arrested in endeavoring to make their escape through Pendleton County to the enemy," Jackson explained. "Those who do not desert will, to some extent, hire substitutes, others will turn out in obedience to the governor's call; but I understand some of them to say they will not 'shoot.' They can be made to fire, but can very easily take bad aim."[168] Despite the obstacles that Jackson confronted, his army increased to about six thousand by mid-April, nearly double of his army's size at Kernstown.[169]

While Jackson reorganized his army, about twenty thousand troops from General Banks's army pushed south up the valley in pursuit of Jackson. Banks moved slowly and cautiously. By mid-April, Banks's army neared Mount Jackson and the van of Stonewall's command under Colonel Ashby. Confidence among the Confederate soldiers reigned supreme, as many believed that so long as Ashby stood between Banks's army and Jackson's main force, they had little cause for anxiety. An officer in the 2nd Virginia Infantry recalled of this confidence: "I never slept more soundly in my life than when in sight of the enemy's camp-fires, with Ashby between us, for I knew that it was well nigh impossible for them to surprise him."[170] Circumstances on April 17 altered that secure feeling when Union cavalry struck and scattered Ashby's command near Mount Jackson. With the Union breakthrough, Jackson now withdrew his command south and the following day arrived in Harrisonburg.[171] Two days later, Jackson marched his army east toward Conrad's Store. From this location, Jackson could establish a strong defense, control Swift Run Gap in the Blue Ridge Mountains (allowing him to maintain a line of communication and reinforcement with Confederate forces on the other side of the Blue Ridge) and give him the capacity to launch attacks against Banks's command.[172]

As Jackson pulled his army to the east into his concealed position at Conrad's Store, General Banks interpreted the movement as a Confederate withdrawal from the valley. On April 19, Banks wired the War Department: "I believe Jackson left this valley yesterday. He is reported to have left Harrisonburg yesterday." Three days later, Banks confirmed his report: "Jackson has abandoned the valley of Virginia permanently, en route, for Gordonsville, by the way of the mountains."[173] Although Banks incorrectly believed that Jackson had left the valley and would no longer pose a threat, something still troubled Banks in mid-April: the numerous supply problems confronted by Union forces in the valley.

Banks believed that the inability of the War Department to properly supply his army was the one factor that prevented a rapid Federal pursuit of Jackson after Kernstown. "The crippled condition of our supplies alone enabled him to escape," Banks lamented to Secretary of War Stanton. "When we halted our troops had not a ration left."[174] An officer in the 2nd Massachusetts noted simply of the supply issues: "Many of the men are barefoot and without rations."[175] While Banks's men waited for the supply wagons, some soldiers in his army relied on the kindness of civilians in the area around New Market. Some officers from the 2nd Massachusetts benefited from the kindness of the Williamson family, who "spread a most bounteous meal" for this group of officers. Despite the Williamsons' Confederate sympathies, their kindness softened some soldiers' attitudes toward Confederate civilians and made it more difficult for some of them to enforce hard war policies. The 2nd Massachusetts' Wilder Dwight observed in a letter home on April 20, 1862: "The general statement that these people are traitors, and deserve all the horrors of civil war, is easy; but the individual case, as it comes up under your eye, showing the helpless family in their dismay at our approach, can hardly fail to excite sympathy."[176]

As General Banks dealt with supply issues, Jackson's force continued to be strengthened. On April 18, Jackson sent a message to General Edward "Old Alleghany" Johnson, who commanded the Army of the Northwest—a small command of about 3,500 men positioned atop Shenandoah Mountain, east of Monterey—to come to his headquarters near Conrad's Store. Jackson ordered Johnson to move his men off Shenandoah Mountain to support his operations in the valley. After the meeting, Johnson sent a message to Colonel John B. Baldwin of the 52nd Virginia Infantry to prepare the Army of the Northwest for the march. The Army of the Northwest's movement to the east began before Johnson reunited with his army. When he reached his command on April 20, Johnson's army had already pulled out of their

General Edward
Johnson. *From* Battles
and Leaders.

positions on Shenandoah Mountain to the village of West View, located six
miles west of the vital rail junction at Staunton.[177]

In addition to the support of Johnson's command, General Robert E.
Lee, then military advisor to President Davis, communicated to Jackson that
he could use General Richard Ewell's division to strike Banks and prevent
Banks from moving east to Fredericksburg to support McClellan's operations
against Richmond. "If you can use Genl. Ewell's division in an attack on
Genl. Banks and to drive him back," Lee instructed Jackson, "it will prove
a great relief to the pressure on Fredericksburg."[178] As much as Lee might
have wanted Jackson to strike Banks, another issue concerned Jackson more
by the end of April: the presence of twenty thousand Union troops under
General John C. Fremont west of the Shenandoah Valley in the Alleghany
Mountains. Since early April, the van of Fremont's army under General
Robert H. Milroy pushed Johnson's Army of the Northwest aggressively.

After Johnson's army, in obedience to Jackson's orders, withdrew east from Shenandoah Mountain, Milroy pushed east to North Mountain, too. Now Milroy—affectionately referred to as "the Gray Eagle" by his men—moved his brigade to within sight of the tracks of the Virginia Central Railroad, Jackson's lifeline to Richmond. If Milroy continued to aggressively push eastward toward Staunton, Jackson's army would be cut off from Richmond. Jackson knew that before he targeted Banks he needed to eliminate the threat to Staunton and even a potential link between Fremont and Banks.

Jackson's plan to deal with the threat west of the valley demonstrated his strategic brilliance. He posted Ewell's division at Conrad's Store. From this location, Ewell could hamper any movement made by Banks. Next, Jackson determined to take his six thousand troops and unite them with Johnson's command—who knew the mountains of western Virginia well—and strike at Fremont's command. Jackson began his movement on April 30, when he marched his men to the east. While initially this provided the appearance of a withdrawal from the valley, Jackson marched his men to Mechum's River Station, boarded the train cars of the Virginia Central Railroad and steamed west toward Staunton. Jackson's force arrived in Staunton on May 4 and combined with Johnson.

Additionally, a contingent of cadets from the Virginia Military Institute joined Jackson's ranks for the expedition. The polished cadets provided a stark contrast to the battle-hardened veterans of Jackson's command. "The spruce equipments and the exact drill of the youths, as they stepped out, full of enthusiasm to take their first actual look upon the horrid visage of war, under their renowned professor," noted one chronicler, "formed a strong contrast with the war-worn and nonchalant veterans who composed the army."[179] On the morning of May 6, Jackson issued orders to his regiments to "cook two days rations, strike tents, and carry so many blankets."[180] None of the soldiers in Jackson's command knew the destination, and speculation ran rampant. "We, as all soldiers," noted a soldier in Jackson's army, "especially when they go without knowing where they are to go, commenced to speculate as to our mysterious movements."[181] On the morning of May 7, Jackson's force, unbeknownst to the men in the ranks, marched west to strike at the van of Fremont's army— General Milroy's brigade positioned in the sleepy hamlet of McDowell.[182]

As Jackson's command marched west, Milroy's scouts confirmed the movement toward McDowell. Milroy fully understood the circumstances that confronted his brigade, and he immediately sent a message to General

Robert Schenck, who commanded a Union brigade at Franklin thirty miles away. By 11:00 a.m. on May 7, Schenck had his brigade underway to support Milroy at McDowell. While Schenck's 1,500-man brigade marched with alacrity to Milroy's aid, the Gray Eagle attempted to slow the Confederate advance by deploying two cannons from the 9th Ohio Battery to Shaw's Ridge. Although the Ohioans had achieved some initial success in slowing one Confederate column, Milroy soon spied another, about two miles distant, to his right. "I ordered a section of the Ninth Ohio Battery...on Shaw's Ridge to shell them and endeavor to retard their progress," Milroy wrote. "This they did with such effect as to cause the enemy to retire beyond the Shenandoah Mountain; but observing another heavy force crossing the mountain on our right, some 2 miles distant, I deemed it prudent to fall back and concentrate at McDowell."[183]

The following morning, Milroy awoke to the sight of Confederates atop Bull Pasture Mountain, less than two miles from McDowell on his right

General Robert H. Milroy.
*Courtesy of the author.*

General Robert Schenck.
*From* Battles and Leaders.

and front. Never one to back down from a fight, Milroy, fearing an attack, decided to disrupt Confederate plans. He ordered his artillery to fire at the positions on Bull Pasture Mountain, while skirmishers deployed to ascertain the strength of the Confederate force.[184] At about 10:00 a.m., reinforcements from Schenck's brigade arrived. This brought the overall strength of the Union force at McDowell to about 3,500 men. Upon his arrival in McDowell, General Schenck assessed the situation and deemed McDowell a horrible place to establish a defense, as the village was surrounded by mountains. "A little observation served to show at once that McDowell, as a defensive position, was entirely untenable," Schenck recalled, "and especially against the largely outnumbering force that was ascertained to be advancing."[185] A paucity of supplies exacerbated the situation for the Federals. Schenck and Milroy both agreed that they had no alternative other than to withdraw from McDowell and join the main body of Fremont's army near Franklin.[186]

Despite their decision to withdraw from McDowell, both generals understood that it presented some challenges. Confederate forces on the heights above McDowell had already observed the Federals, and neither Union commander believed that Jackson would permit them to leave without a fight. Moreover, Milroy and Schenck felt that they would not have done their duty as soldiers if they did not at least attempt to test the Confederate position. "Such a movement, however, could not with any safety or propriety be commenced before night," Schenck observed, "nor did it seem advisable to undertake it without first ascertaining or feeling the actual strength of the rebel force before us."[187] Both officers also wanted to do something that would limit the capacity of the enemy to pursue the retreating brigades to Franklin. General Schenck believed that some type of offensive activity "would serve to check or disable him from his full power or disposition to pursue."[188]

Throughout the day, while Milroy and Schenck looked to the details of their withdrawal, Confederates from General Johnson's command fortified positions on Bull Pasture Mountain atop an imposing eminence known as Sitlington's Hill. Initially, this did nothing to heighten the consternation among the Union command; however, when Captain George R. Latham of the 2nd Virginia (U.S.) informed Milroy that "the rebels were endeavoring to plant a battery upon the mountain" anxieties increased rapidly.[189] If Confederate artillery posted itself atop Bull Pasture Mountain, both Union brigades faced imminent annihilation. Milroy promptly went to Schenck—his superior in seniority on the field that day—and implored him to permit him to make "a reconnaissance for the purpose of obtaining accurate information of their strength and position."[190] Schenck approved Milroy's request. With five regiments—the 25th, 32nd, 75th and 82nd Ohio and 3rd Virginia (U.S.)—Milroy executed his "reconnaissance." With about 1,700 men in this force, Milroy's operation resembled an assault more than a scouting mission. Regardless of the report that Milroy received, the Confederates had no intentions of planting guns atop Sitlington's Hill, as the steepness of the slope made it difficult to even get infantry to the crest. Additionally, one of Jackson's staff officers explained that Jackson did not want to place artillery atop Sitlington's Hill, as there was no easy way to pull the guns from the position in the event that Union regiments broke the Confederate line.[191] The Confederate brigades atop Sitlington's Hill held the utmost confidence, regardless of the absence of artillery, that no Union commander would dare attack their position. Colonel W.C. Scott, who commanded Johnson's second brigade, prepared his men for an attack but did not believe that a threat would ever manifest itself. "Col. Scott formed his line of battle on the crest of the hill, and his men faced west. This was a mere prevention to guard against attack," recalled one Confederate, "which he did not expect."[192] Officers such as Scott, however, did not fully realize General Milroy's fearlessness.

As Milroy marched his command across the rain-swollen Bull Pasture River, he believed that the only way to guarantee the safety of the Union command from Confederate artillery was to attack Sitlington's Hill. The 25th and 75th Ohio "advanced in the most gallant manner up the face of the hill" and struck near the Confederate left. The two Ohio regiments attacked "most splendidly," in Milroy's estimation, "received and returned the enemy fire with such spirit."[193] Colonel Scott and his Virginians appeared stunned at the Union assault. Some of his soldiers initially broke under the shock of the attack. In a dangerous situation, Scott waved his hat furiously and urged his men to rally. "Scott's situation was then perilous in the extreme," reported a Richmond newspaper. "He placed himself on his line of battle before his men with not more than a dozen men who had not left, and waving his hat around his head, appealed to his men in the most animating manner to rally to his support. He asked them if Virginians would let a parcel of Yankees make them run on their own soil?"[194]

While the attack commenced against the left, Milroy's three other regiments struck the right. He ordered the 32nd and 82nd Ohio and 3rd Virginia (U.S.) to "turn the right flank of the enemy, and, if possible, attack them in the rear."[195] Some of Milroy's soldiers in this attack column could not believe the order. "It was now determined to not only risk an engagement, but to attack the enemy in a very strong position…on the top of Bull Pasture Mountain—a position almost impregnable if defended with reasonable skill and courage," observed a veteran of the 32nd Ohio. "It was a position that should not have been attacked at all."[196] Nonetheless, the assault commenced. The initial assault up Sitlington's Hill presented an almost surreal experience to some of Milroy's soldiers, who heard the battle and saw the scenes but still could not make sense of the battle's reality. Alfred Lee, a soldier in the 82nd Ohio, noted that as his regiment surged forward in "exhilaration," he looked to the rear and noticed that some of the men in the regiment were lying down. "My first impression was that they had lain down to avoid being hit," Lee recalled. "But they were motionless. The truth flashed over me—they were dead!"[197] Other soldiers in Milroy's brigade understood the moment's severity, but some were also reminded that this conflict had truly pitted brother against brother and friend against friend. When soldiers from the

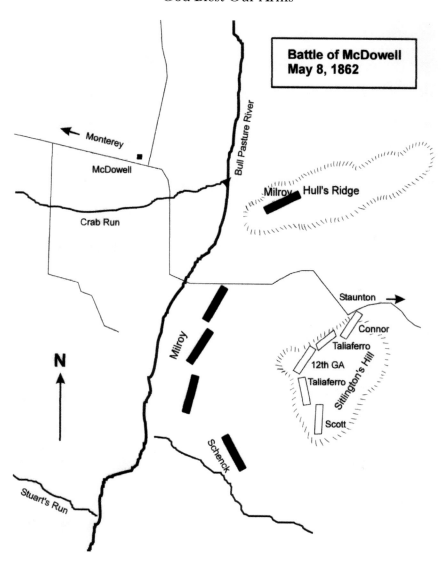

Map of the Battle of McDowell. *Courtesy of the author.*

3rd Virginia (U.S.) came within earshot of the Confederate line, they shouted at the troops in the 31st Virginia. Both regiments had been raised in the area around Clarksburg, Virginia—Stonewall Jackson's birthplace—and many knew one another.[198]

Despite Sitlington's apparent commanding nature, two issues concerned General Johnson about his capacity to defend the heights. First, Johnson worried about the center of his line held by the 12th Georgia. The center jutted out toward the Union attack columns like a nose and was susceptible to fire from not only the front but from both flanks as well.[199]

Second, Milroy made Johnson's situation more tenable when he placed two Union cannon atop Hull's Hill—a piece of high ground adjoining Sitlington's Hill.[200] Despite the situation, Johnson's men, particularly the 12th Georgia, did all they could to slow Milroy's assault. A Virginian who watched the Georgians defend the Confederate center, noted: "The brave old Twelfth Georgia stood like heroes of many battles…may it be said of those gallant Georgians that they deserve the honor and praise of all admirers of true bravery and gallantry…They know no fear—they enter a battle not to be conquered but to conquer."[201]

As the Georgians stood their ground, both Johnson and Stonewall Jackson worried that they would not be able to hold on their own. Jackson sent General William Taliaferro's brigade to support Johnson's center. Taliaferro's men arrived and aided the Georgians in forcing back Milroy's assault, albeit momentarily.[202] Never known to back down from a fight, Milroy reorganized his command and struck again. By this point in the battle, the sun had begun to set. As daylight diminished, the Union attack columns had a decided advantage.

Due to the steepness of Sitlington's slopes, the Confederate defenders had to stand to deliver their volleys into their attackers. As they stood up, their bodies became silhouetted against the sky and made easier targets for Milroy's men, who were cloaked in an ethereal atmosphere of darkness, smoke, trees and bushes. Milroy's infantry poured volleys into whatever attracted their gaze, including pockets of bushes that through the din of battle were mistaken as Confederates. "The enemy had come and so often had our men exposed against the clear sky line," recorded one of Jackson's veterans. "This accounted for the extraordinary splintered condition of the thorn bushes on the hill, which must have looked to them like men or groups of them."[203] As total darkness descended over the battleground, and Union soldiers exhausted their ammunition supplies, the Federal commanders in McDowell had no other alternative than to quit the field. "The evening also was well advanced," recalled the 75th Ohio's Colonel Nathaniel McLean, "so that our men could only see the enemy by the flashes of their guns. The moon was shining, but did not give sufficient light to enable the men to shoot with accuracy."[204] By 8:30 p.m., the Federals withdrew into the village of McDowell.

As the Federals gathered in McDowell, some of the men in Milroy's command petitioned to remain in position and renew the attack in the morning. Although tempted to remain and fight, Milroy "deemed it prudent...to withdraw them."[205] Throughout the night, the Federal commanders made preparations to pull out. Union officers ordered their men to destroy whatever supplies could not be carried, to prevent them from falling into Confederate hands. Thousands of musket cartridges were thrown into a stream, while structures housing foodstuffs were burned. Some residents of McDowell also reported that the Union soldiers pressed some of their livestock into the army's service to evacuate the artillery.[206] About 2:00 a.m. on May 9, after having destroyed as much as possible, the Union command withdrew to the west to join the main body of Fremont's army near Franklin.[207] When Confederates entered the Union camps the following morning, they found the "pebbly bottom of the neighboring stream...strewn with tens of thousands of musket-cartridges, and vast heaps of bread [that] were still smoking amidst the ashes of the store-houses which had sheltered them."[208]

Although Milroy had "to fall back before traitors," the fighting prowess of the Federals at McDowell buoyed his spirits. In his official report of the engagement, written less than one week after the battle, Milroy praised his troops. "From 3 p.m. until 8 o'clock our small force engaged with undaunted bravery a force of the enemy," Milroy reported, "and maintained the position from which they had driven them, displaying a courage and zeal which has merited the thanks of the country and proved them true representatives of the American citizen soldier."[209] Likewise, General Schenck reveled in the gallantry displayed by the Union troops at McDowell. "No veteran troops, I am sure, ever acquitted themselves with more ardor," Schenck penned, "and yet with such order and coolness, as they displayed in marching and fighting up that steep mountain side in the face of a hot and incessant fire."[210] While Milroy and Schenck heaped praise on their men, they also would have taken additional comfort in knowing that the Federals inflicted more casualties on the Confederates than suffered by the Union command. The Federals lost 259 men at McDowell, whereas the Confederates suffered 416 casualties.[211] Among the Confederate casualties was General Johnson, who received a wound to his ankle.[212]

After darkness ended the assaults, the Confederates tended to their wounded. Again the rugged terrain presented problems, as it precluded ambulances from coming up Sitlington's Hill to evacuate the wounded. "This place was so rugged and steep that…we [could not] get an ambulance to the battlefield. We had to carry the wounded down a steep, rocky hollow," recorded a veteran of the Stonewall Brigade, "and it took us nearly all night to do so."[213] To veterans who walked the battlefield afterward, the scenes shocked them. Major Frank B. Jones of the Stonewall Brigade exclaimed, "O, the dead! The dying! The screams of the wounded! I have never seen so much of it. I was deeply affected."[214]

While some Confederate soldiers and doctors cared for the wounded, Jackson prepared the main elements of his army to pursue the retreating Federals and block any possible routes for Fremont's army to link with Banks's command in the Shenandoah Valley. To prevent the linkup between Fremont and Banks, Jackson turned to his talented mapmaker Jedediah Hotchkiss. Jackson directed Hotchkiss to take a body of Confederate cavalry and block the mountain passes into the Shenandoah Valley. Hotchkiss's detachment did all it could to erect impediments, including felling trees, burning bridges and blocking roads with large stones.[215]

Meanwhile, Jackson took the main body of his valley army and pursued. The pursuit proved difficult, however, as Milroy had ordered the woods along the retreat path to be set on fire. If Jackson wanted to pursue and catch the Federals, his army would need to push through an inferno to achieve its objective. "Milroy, like the bull of Southern woodlands," noted one of Jackson's veterans, "which seeks shelter from mosquitoes in the friendly folds of smoke, fired the mountains right and left as he retreated."[216] Jackson's men pressed forward, and by May 12, Jackson's men had caught up with the Federal force near Franklin.

What Jackson discovered, however, did not please him at all. Once Schenck and Milroy had completed their withdrawal to Franklin, the Union commanders placed their men on high ground that commanded the surrounding country. Through the smoke and fire, Union artillery opened on Jackson's column. "We followed in hot pursuit as far as Franklin," remembered one of Jackson's veterans. "There the enemy took position in a narrow valley that ran between the mountain hills; these hills were covered with woods, and they had fired the woods on both sides of the valley in their front, and as soon as we came in sight, their artillery commenced firing on us. We could not locate the guns because of the smoke."[217] Despite his desire to crush the Union force, Jackson achieved his mission of preventing a junction between Fremont's forces and Banks's army while also protecting the vital rail center at Staunton. With nothing else to gain strategically, Jackson headed back to the Shenandoah Valley. "The junction between Banks and Milroy [Fremont] having been prevented," Jackson explained of his decision to pull back from Franklin, "and becoming satisfied of the impracticability of capturing the defeated enemy, owing to the mountainous character of the country being favorable for a retreating army to make its escape, I determined…that I would not attempt to press farther, but return to the open country of the Shenandoah Valley."[218]

With the immediate threat from Fremont's army eliminated, Jackson sent a note to Richmond that announced his victory at McDowell. In Jackson's typical style, he claimed no personal credit for the success but rather gave all credit to God. "God blest our arms with victory at McDowell Station," Jackson informed Richmond. Despite the message's brevity, it had a profound impact on the Confederacy, as news of Jackson's success had been the only good news that the Confederate nation received in early May 1862. With the loss at Shiloh, the capture of New Orleans and the capital threatened, Jackson's success at McDowell provided optimism to a people who had every reason to feel hopeless. "This announcement was received by the people of Virginia and of the Confederate States with peculiar delight," remembered one of Jackson's staff officers, "because it was the first blush of the returning day of triumphs after a season of gloomy disasters."[219]

While the Confederacy reveled in Jackson's success at McDowell, Jackson wanted his command to thank God for the victory. Jackson proclaimed May 12 as a day of Thanksgiving and prayer in his army. "I congratulate you on your recent victory at McDowell," Jackson informed his soldiers. "I request you to unite with me…in thanksgiving to Almighty God for thus having crowned your arms with success, and in praying that He will continue to lead you on from victory to victory, until our independence shall be established, and make us that people whose God is the Lord."[220] Regimental chaplains held prayer services at 10:00 a.m., and soldiers in Jackson's army turned their attention, for the moment, away from war and to God. "With the blue and towering mountains covered with the verdure of Spring…that army," noted a Confederate soldier of the prayer service, "equipped for the stern conflict of war, bent in humble praise and thanksgiving to the God of Battles for the success vouchsafed to our arms."[221]

By May 15, Jackson's army had departed from their camps near Franklin and made their way back to the Shenandoah Valley. Some Federal soldiers seemed pleased at the news that Jackson had withdrawn his men to the east, but Milroy was not one of them. Always aggressive, Milroy urged Fremont to pursue Jackson, but Fremont would not allow it. Milroy complained to his wife: "I fear I shall not like Fremont, he is not sufficiently free, sociable, and approachable for me, and he don't dash on after the rebels in a style to suit me."[222] Despite Milroy's criticisms, Fremont's decision to not pursue proved wise. With his army concentrated at Franklin, Fremont's army now rested nearly sixty miles from its supply base at New Creek. With the absence of rail lines between the two points and only one wagon road, which had become nearly impassable due to recent rains, Fremont's already ill-supplied army could not afford to pursue Jackson.[223] With Fremont's army in a state of paralysis near Franklin, Jackson next set his sights on General Banks in the Shenandoah Valley. For his campaign against Banks, Jackson would need, in the estimation of one Confederate veteran, "energy, nerve, rapidity of movement, and all the greatest faculties of the soldier."[224]

# Chapter 4

# "THE VICTORY WAS COMPLETE AND GLORIOUS"

As Stonewall Jackson's troops marched back into the Shenandoah Valley following McDowell, General Lee sent Jackson a dispatch urging him to strike General Banks immediately. By mid-May, Lee learned that General Shields's division of Banks's corps had been ordered from the valley. Lee guessed Shields's destination but ultimately believed that it would in some way be utilized to support McClellan's operations against Richmond. Lee's estimation proved correct, as Shields's men made their way to Fredericksburg. Additionally, Lee informed Jackson that Banks's army no longer stood at Harrisonburg but rather had pulled back north to Strasburg. This movement also raised some questions in Lee's mind as to Banks's ultimate objective. "Banks has fallen back on Strasburg... Whatever may be Banks' intention it is very desirable to prevent him from going either to Fredericksburg or to the Peninsula," Lee informed Jackson, "a successful blow struck at him would delay, if it does not prevent, his moving to either place."[225] Despite Lee's directive to strike Banks, he reminded Jackson that operations in the valley were secondary and that if any part of his forces were needed for the defense of Richmond, he would have to relinquish them. "But you will not, in any demonstrations you may make in that direction," Lee reminded Jackson, "lose sight of the fact that it may become necessary for you to come to the support of Genl. Johnston, and hold yourself in readiness to do so if required."[226]

With this directive, Jackson took immediate steps to put his offensive plans against Banks in motion. On May 17, Jackson, as his army closed in on

Harrisonburg, ordered Ewell to move his division toward Luray to maintain a keen eye on Banks and stop him should he try to move across the Blue Ridge. Ewell also received a dispatch earlier that day from General Johnston, who advised against attacking Banks and instead wanted Ewell's division sent to Richmond's defense. The contradictory orders frustrated Ewell.

Although the array of dispatches bothered Ewell, it had been something that had become commonplace during his short tenure in the Shenandoah Valley. Lee, Johnston and Jackson had all been guilty of sending Ewell orders that contradicted other directives. What further frustrated Ewell was the ambiguity of some of Jackson's communiqués throughout May. For example, when Jackson marched to crush Milroy at McDowell, he did not inform Ewell of the larger mission. Jackson's unwillingness to share the complete picture with his subordinates aggravated Ewell, who at various times during the first several weeks of May vented his frustration in front of his division. "I remember well [Ewell]…cursing about Jackson having gone off without leaving orders for him or telling him where he was going," recalled a soldier in Ewell's command. "It was a most unfortunate position for Gen. Ewell… Gen. Jackson was then looked upon as a wild, reckless fighter."[227] Ewell stated simply of Jackson in early May: "He is crazy as a March hare…I tell you, sir, he is crazy."[228]

Fed up with contradictory orders from his superiors, Ewell decided to leave his division and ride to Jackson's camp in Mount Solon. There the two generals discussed the strategic situation and, according to an officer in Jackson's army, "decided upon the plan for a most energetic pursuit of Banks."[229]

Once Ewell determined to remain with Jackson, the remainder of the plan seemed simple enough. Jackson and Ewell would combine forces—bringing Jackson's command to about seventeen thousand troops—and then move north to strike Banks.[230] Although the concept seemed straightforward, Jackson knew that in order to carry out his offensive strategy his men needed to march at a rapid pace. "Hours to him," noted a Confederate soldier in Jackson's command, "were as days to other commanders."[231]

In the early morning hours of May 19, Jackson's march began. With speed a necessity, he ordered his men to leave behind unnecessary equipment, including knapsacks, that would slow them down. Although Jackson did not share his plans with his soldiers, the order to leave their knapsacks behind portended a major movement. A veteran of the Stonewall Brigade noted

General Richard Ewell.
*From* Battles and Leaders.

simply: "We knew there was some game on hand then, for when General Jackson ordered knapsacks to be left behind he meant business."[232] All seemed to be going smoothly for Jackson during the first day; however, that all changed on the following day, when General Ewell reached Jackson's camp near New Market. Ewell delivered a dispatch he received from General Johnston formally recalling the division to Richmond. Although incensed at the moment, another message received later in the day from Johnston gave Jackson control of Ewell's division if it could be used to crush Banks. "The whole question is, whether or not General Jackson and yourself are too late to attack Banks," Johnston wrote Ewell, "If so the march eastward should be made. If not (supposing your strength sufficient) then attack."[233]

On the morning of May 21, Jackson's men marched north into New Market. Jackson gave every indication that he would march his army north to strike Banks via the Valley Pike. However, when the column came to Cross Street, Jackson motioned his men to turn to the right. Leading Jackson's column was General Richard Taylor's brigade from Ewell's division. When Taylor turned his men to the east and headed toward the New Market Gap in the Massanutten Mountain, Taylor was confused. Of all the brigades in Ewell's division, Jackson ordered Ewell to keep all of them, except Taylor's, on the east side of Massanutten and send only Taylor's command to the main valley. Taylor, who did not fully comprehend his role in Jackson's attempt to confuse Banks, could not fathom why Jackson ordered him to march west across the Massanutten and then back east over the course of two days. Jovially, Taylor wrote after the war: "I began to think Jackson was an unconscious poet, and, as an ardent lover of nature, desired to give strangers an opportunity to admire the beauties of his Valley."[234] Jackson's plan now came into focus: Jackson would unite with Ewell at Luray, and then the combined force would march north, down the Luray Valley, and first strike Banks's strategic left flank at Front Royal, an important depot along the Manassas Gap Railroad and Banks's lifeline.[235]

While Jackson set his plan in motion, General Banks worried tremendously about his army's condition. By the time Banks's army was concentrated at Strasburg in mid-May, his army's strength had been diminished dramatically. Banks's command had fewer than ten thousand men.[236] Numerous, previously published, accounts of this portion of the Valley Campaign usually portray Banks as an inept commander who placed his small army in a precarious situation, totally oblivious to the dangers that Jackson's army presented. For example, Millard Bushong in his *General Turner Ashby and Stonewall's Valley Campaign* states that Banks "did not seem to fear the approaching Confederates."[237] Conclusions such as these are unwarranted and incorrect. Although Banks was a political general who did not possess a military ability equivalent to Jackson's, he understood the situation extremely well in mid-May.

Within days after his arrival in Strasburg, General Banks worried tremendously about his capacity to defend against any Confederate attack. "The return of the rebel forces of General Jackson to the valley, after his forced march against Milroy and Schenck, increases my anxiety," Banks wired the War Department, "for the safety of the position I occupy and

Union troops in Front Royal in the spring of 1862. *Courtesy of the author.*

that of the troops under my command...I am compelled to believe that he meditates attack here."[238]

Despite Banks's anxieties, Secretary of War Edwin Stanton further hampered Banks's efforts to protect his command at Strasburg when he ordered Banks on May 16 to stretch his command from Strasburg east to Front Royal so that it could protect the Manassas Gap Railroad between Strasburg and Front Royal. Banks obeyed and sent about one thousand men under Colonel John R. Kenly to garrison Front Royal, a place deemed as an "indefensible position" by Banks.[239] Although he carried out Stanton's directive, Banks warned on the afternoon of May 16: "This will reduce my force greatly, which is already too small to defend Strasburg if attacked."[240]

Over the course of the next several days, Banks implored the War Department for assistance. "We are preparing defenses as rapidly as possible," Banks wrote to Stanton, "but with the best aid of this character my force is insufficient to meet the enemy in such strength as he will certainly come, if he attacks us at all, and our situation certainly invites attack in the strongest manner."[241] Banks requested that the War Department send him an artillery battery of twenty-pound Parrot rifles that could be placed in Strasburg's defenses. Banks also requested infantry reinforcements. "My infantry should be increased," Banks explained, "both for the defense of the town and the protection of the railway and bridges."[242] So adamant had Banks become about being reinforced that he sent his adjutant, Major R. Morris Copeland, to Washington, D.C., to appeal to Stanton directly. Still, the expressed concern fell on deaf ears, and Stanton denied the request for support, as he did not believe that Jackson presented a major threat to Banks.[243]

Banks fumed with indignation at Stanton's assessment. The Union commander fully understood that Jackson would do whatever he could to hold onto the valley and continue his mission of diversion. "To these important considerations ought to be added the persistent adherence of Jackson to the defense of the valley," Banks observed, "and his well-known purpose to expel the Government troops from this country if in his power. This may be assumed as certain. There is probably no more fixed and determined purpose in the whole circle of the enemy's plans."[244] Stanton refused to send support. In both his estimation as well as that of President Lincoln, the important operations were against Richmond, not in the Shenandoah Valley. One of Banks's staff officers, valley native David Hunter Strother, clearly understood the situation, as he penned in his journal: "I fear the Department of the Shenandoah is no longer to be the theatre of glorious deeds. The neighborhood of Richmond is now the great center of interest."[245]

Despite Banks's concerns, some of the soldiers in his command held little apprehension. A veteran of the 3rd Wisconsin noted once the army fell back to Strasburg: "Here we made some little show of fortifying, but in the main, we were as easy and unconcerned as though the war was over…In camp, bets were freely offered, with no takers, that the regiment would be back in Wisconsin by September."[246] This soldier's optimistic assessment soon proved false.

While Banks lamented his situation and prepared his defenses as best as possible, Jackson's column set its sights on Front Royal. By the early morning of May 23, Jackson's columns rested within about ten miles of Front Royal. While his army marched north, Jackson sent Colonel Turner Ashby's cavalry to Buckton Station to disrupt the lines of communication between Front Royal and Strasburg. Ashby carried out his mission successfully, crushed the small Union garrison there, and severed the lines of communication between Banks in Strasburg and Kenly's command in Front Royal.[247]

As Ashby's cavalry performed their mission at Buckton, Jackson rode ahead of his main column on the Luray Road and halted at Asbury Chapel—located about three miles south of Front Royal's Union pickets. Jackson assessed the situation and felt uncomfortable attacking Front Royal on the Luray Road, as there was no way to conceal his command and maintain the element of surprise. Jackson soon learned, however, from Isaac King, a leader at Asbury Chapel, that one of the men in Jackson's army—Lieutenant Samuel Simpson, a native of the area—might be able to suggest another route. Jackson immediately summoned Simpson. The valley native suggested Jackson move the army on Snake Road, which followed a path to the northeast into the Blue Ridge Mountains and formed an intersection with the Gooney Manor Road. Once on the Gooney Manor Road, Jackson could deploy his army and strike the small garrison at Front Royal.[248] Jackson agreed.

As his army neared Asbury Chapel, Jackson learned that the primary force in Front Royal was Kenly's 1st Maryland. Immediately Jackson summoned the 1st Maryland from his army to move to the front of the column and lead the attack. "General Jackson's order that our regiment should take the front and make the assault on the town was due to the discovery that it was occupied by the First Maryland Federal Regiment," recalled a Maryland Confederate. "He thus put us on our mettle to show which were the best men and the truest representatives of Maryland."[249] When Colonel Bradley Johnson, who commanded the regiment, received Jackson's order, he was dealing with a potential mutiny in the regiment. Some of the men's enlistments had expired, and they simply refused to fight. Johnson lambasted his men for refusing to fight; however, when they received the order from Jackson, many of the men in the regiment rejoined and moved to the head of the column to lead the assault against their fellow Marylanders.[250] "Bradley Johnson made a stirring appeal to some…men who had refused to do duty," recalled a Marylander, but the appeal and Jackson's request for the Marylanders to move to the front of the column prompted them to take "up their arms again."[251]

At the same time as Jackson's men climbed the Snake Road, Colonel Kenly's unsuspecting garrison rested comfortably in Front Royal. At about 1:00 p.m., however, that all changed when an unidentified African American man rode into Kenly's lines and informed the Federals that "the

Colonel Bradley T. Johnson. *From* Battles and Leaders.

Colonel John Kenly. *From* The Soldier in Our Civil War, *1885.*

rebels were coming in great numbers, and they will surround you, and cut you off."[252] Some of Kenly's troops did not believe the report. Kenly, however, did not discount it. "As soon, however, as Colonel Kenly saw the man he became satisfied of the Rebels approach," noted one observer. "The long roll was beaten, the men responded springing hastily to their arms, and forming in line."[253]

Belle Boyd, the famed Confederate spy with a penchant for self-promotion and historical embellishment, recorded that she noticed the Federal garrison in Front Royal making preparations for an attack. At that moment, Boyd decided to find the Confederates and give them information about Front Royal's defenders. In a dark blue dress with a white apron, Boyd ran into the Confederate lines waving her hands frantically. One of Jackson's staff officers, Henry Kyd Douglas, observed that Boyd "waved a bonnet as she came on." Douglas called Jackson's attention to Boyd. She confirmed Jackson's suspicions that only a small Union force guarded Front Royal.[254]

While Jackson made his final preparations, Kenly determined to delay Jackson as long as possible. Heavily outnumbered, Kenly never imagined that he would defeat Jackson, but he hoped that he could delay the Confederate army long enough to evacuate the supplies in Front Royal; more importantly, he wanted to prevent Jackson from moving west toward the Valley Pike and cutting off Banks from Winchester and his line of retreat across the Potomac River. The *Sun*, a Baltimore newspaper, reported of Kenly's decision to block Jackson's advance: "Colonel Kenly, in a cool and collected manner, made an address to his command…he…told them to retreat at that moment would be certain death…To this the men responded with a cheer that they would stand and fight."[255] "Colonel Kenly at once prepared to hold the position at all hazards," remembered a veteran of the 1st Maryland (U.S.), "being fully aware that if he did not check the enemy's progress the severance of General Banks' line of retreat to the Potomac was inevitable."[256] Simultaneously with his preparations to block Jackson, Kenly sent a courier—Sergeant C.H. Greenleaf from the 5th New York Cavalry—to alert Banks of the approach of Jackson's army.[257]

At about 2:00 p.m., Jackson's column slammed into Kenly's pickets. With only three men on this post, Jackson's men easily swept them aside and pushed into Front Royal. Kenly utilized his small command as best as he could. He leaned heavily on the two guns of Knap's Pennsylvania Battery commanded by Lieutenant Charles Atwell to slow the Confederate

Belle Boyd. *Courtesy of the Library of Congress.*

onslaught; however, holding on to the town proved difficult. Within an hour from the time of the assault, Jackson cleared Kenly's defenders from Front Royal.[258] When the Confederates rushed into the town, they were greeted with great enthusiasm by the overwhelming Confederate civilian population. One Maryland Confederate noted that a young girl, about fifteen years old, rushed out of her home oblivious to the flying bullets and shouted, "Go it boys! Maryland whip Maryland!"[259] The young Thomas Ashby, a resident of Front Royal who had been swimming in a creek when the battle began, noted of the scene: "The return of the Confederates so cheered our people that they opened their hearts and homes to the soldiers with joyful welcome and dispensed lavish hospitality."[260] "Women and children," recalled one of Jackson's soldiers, "wild with delight and gratitude, some with tears in their eyes, welcomed us as their deliverers. I never felt the bliss of aiding my fellow men so much as then."[261]

Not all of Front Royal's civilians greeted the Confederates enthusiastically, however. The town's Unionist sympathizers and African Americans trembled at the presence of Jackson's army. "The servants are disappointed and furious beyond mere words at the treatment their Yankee friends have received at the hands of 'Rebels,'" noted a resident of Front Royal. "They don't say anything but are so sullen. The surprise was evidently very great and very disagreeable."[262]

Although most civilians reveled in the victory, and the soldiers enjoyed their reception, Jackson did not want to merely capture Front Royal—he desired to crush Kenly's command. Throughout the afternoon, Kenly's men retreated north, with Jackson on their heels. By late afternoon, Kenly's men pulled back across both forks of the Shenandoah River. Once across, Kenly posted Atwell's two cannons atop Guard Hill to slow the enemy assault. To further diminish Jackson's capacity to pursue, Kenly ordered the bridges over the forks of the Shenandoah burned. The attempt to destroy the bridge over the South Fork of the Shenandoah River failed, however; Sergeant William Taylor, of the 1st Maryland (U.S.), although wounded, destroyed enough of the bridge over the North Fork to dramatically slow the Confederate pursuit. Taylor, who performed another heroic act at Weldon Railroad in August 1864, received the Medal of Honor in 1897 for his gallant actions at Front Royal.[263]

Jackson, fearing that this might allow Kenly to escape, ordered Lieutenant Colonel Thomas S. Flournoy's 6th Virginia Cavalry to pursue. According to various accounts, some of the Virginia troopers eased their way across the charred remains of the bridge over the North Fork, while others forded the river.[264] Several miles north of Front Royal, Kenly established his final defensive line at Cedarville near Fairview—the home of Thomas McKay.[265] This location had to be the spot of Kenly's last stand, as it marked the final point that he could block Confederate forces from moving west, gaining access to the Valley Pike and cutting off Banks from Winchester. Despite his best intentions and efforts, Kenly's men could not equal the force of Flournoy's troopers. When it became apparent that the Marylanders would not be able to have any success against the Virginia horsemen, they stripped their regimental standard from its staff and divided the fragments among the veterans.[266] As confusion dominated the field, Kenly received two wounds—one to the head and another to his arm. Incapacitated, Kenly, along with nine hundred other soldiers from his command, fell captive to

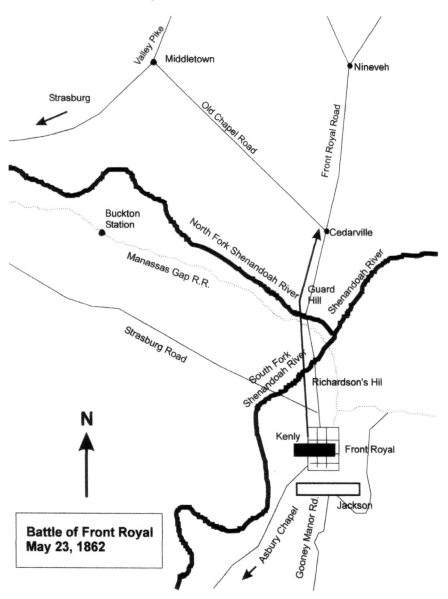

Map of the Battle of Front Royal. *Courtesy of the author.*

the Confederates.[267] While the Federal force suffered catastrophic losses, the cost in Jackson's command proved minimal, with fewer than fifty casualties.

The day after Kenly's defeat and capture, Colonel Bradley Johnson visited Kenly and inquired if there was anything he could do for the fellow Marylander. Kenly declined. In the decades that followed, Kenly's and Johnson's paths would cross multiple times as the two became good friends. In many ways, their postwar friendship stood as a symbol of postwar reconciliation among former enemies. During the Confederate Memorial Day ceremonies in Winchester in June 1880, Johnson presented Kenly with a garrison flag captured by Johnson's troops during the Battle of Front Royal. With Stonewall Jackson's widow Mary Anna in attendance, the participants regarded it as a "touching scene."[268] Eleven years later, Johnson attended Kenly's funeral as an honorary pallbearer.[269]

About two weeks after Kenly's fight at Front Royal, the Confederates paroled him due to the severity of his wounds. When he returned home to Baltimore, Kenly was welcomed as a hero. Newspapers in the North referred to Kenly as "the hero of the Front Royal battle."[270] In August, President Lincoln promoted Kenly to brigadier general for his conduct at the battle.[271]

While Kenly battled Jackson at Front Royal, General Banks had little inclination that his force had been attacked until about 5:00 p.m. According to one of Banks's staff officers at about that time, an unidentified African American male rode to Banks's headquarters in Strasburg and informed him of Kenly's fate. Soon other reports began to trickle in to Banks's headquarters. Now the commanding general needed to make a decision to either remain at Strasburg and fight or retreat north to Winchester. Most accounts of this portion of the campaign portray Banks as very confused and indecisive. Colonel George Gordon, one of Banks's brigade commanders, has been the main source of that criticism. An 1846 graduate of West Point—the same class in which Stonewall Jackson graduated—Gordon despised the political General Banks. When Gordon published his *Brook Farm to Cedar Mountain* in 1885, he was intensely critical of Banks's handling of the situation in the valley. Historians from G.F.R. Henderson until more modern scholars have relied heavily on Gordon's portrayal of Banks to solidify the notion that he was indecisive; however, Gordon's account is self-serving at times and does not provide the truest analysis of events.[272] In his postwar account, Gordon states that on the evening of May 23 Banks did nothing to secure his army's massive amount of supplies and either prepare a defense at Strasburg or prepare to move his army to Winchester. Gordon stated that he went to Banks's headquarters and found Banks "brooding over thoughts he did not reveal; he was spiritless and dejected."[273]

Accounts of David Hunter Strother, written at the time, paint a different image of General Banks. According to Strother, Banks gave orders to pack up his stores at Strasburg within hours after he received news of the attack at Front Royal. "There was some commotion and general sending of orders to pack up," Strother noted in his journal.[274] Although Banks had ordered his army to pack and prepare for a movement northward, he decided to remain at Strasburg for the moment. Gordon characterized Banks's decision to remain at Strasburg as a manifestation of his fear. The brigade commander believed that Banks had determined to hold at Strasburg because a withdrawal would show the Union general's timidity. "The thought so long the subject of his meditation was at last out. General Banks was afraid of being thought afraid."[275] Evidence suggests otherwise. Banks received a directive from the War Department to remain at Strasburg, as reinforcements were on the way. "Arrangements are making to send you ample re-enforcements. Do not give up the ship before succor can arrive," the War Department directed Banks.[276]

Valley native David Hunter Strother provided valuable service to General Banks during the 1862 Valley Campaign and countered Colonel George Gordon's negative portrayal of Banks's handling of the situation after Front Royal. *Courtesy of the Library of Congress.*

Circumstances on the morning of May 24, however, caused Banks to decide against remaining at Strasburg and pull back to Winchester. During the late night hours of May 23 and early morning hours of May 24, Captain Charles H.T. Collis took a detachment from his Zouaves d'Afrique on a reconnaissance mission toward Front Royal. When Collis returned to Banks's headquarters on the morning of the twenty-fourth, he informed Banks that Jackson's army was in full force. In anticipation of the worst, Banks had already begun to move the sick soldiers of his command north to Winchester.[277] "I concluded that the safest course for my command," Banks informed the War Department on May 24, "was to anticipate the enemy in the occupation of Winchester."[278] A withdrawal to Winchester also meant that Banks would have the advantage of additional infantry support from the 10th Maine, as well as four cavalry companies en route to Winchester from Harpers Ferry.[279]

As Banks put his column in motion toward Winchester, Jackson moved his command west toward the Valley Pike and General Banks. Jackson, however, did not know Banks's precise location and feared that if Banks got to Winchester that the Union army would be able to escape from the valley. In order to annihilate Banks, Jackson needed to block the Valley Pike at some point south of Winchester. The quickest route from Jackson's position north of Front Royal to the Valley Pike was the Old Chapel Road (present-day Reliance Road), which intersected the Valley Pike at Middletown. While Jackson took the main body of his army toward Middletown, a detachment of cavalry under Brigadier General George H. Steuart made its way to the Valley Pike at Newtown (present-day Stephens City), five miles north of Middletown, "with instructions to observe the movements of the enemy at that point."[280]

About 9:00 a.m. on May 24, Banks's column of about five thousand soldiers and five hundred wagons rolled northward on the Valley Pike toward Winchester. Strasburg's ardently pro-Confederate civilian population used the opportunity to express their displeasure toward the Union soldiers. The civilians of Strasburg "were not afraid to come out and look," recalled a veteran of the 5th Connecticut, "leer and jeer at you as you passed; and the women would be all at once turned to bitterness…The dogs, too, seemed to be altogether more numerous at every house."[281] As the column moved north, Banks and his staff stood near the bridge over Cedar Creek on the Valley Pike. Banks hoped that his army could move fast enough before

Jackson spied the movement. Hope turned to despair when Banks received news late that morning that Confederate cavalry blocked the Valley Pike at Newtown. Now Banks feared that he might have to pull his men back to Strasburg and fight. To prepare for this contingency, Banks ordered Captain James W. Abert of the topographical corps to work with Collis's Zouaves d'Afrique to prepare a fire to burn the bridge over Cedar Creek so that Jackson would not be able to pursue. Obediently, Abert went to the nearby Stickley Farm and "procured a tar-barrel, some straw, some commissary pork, and other flammable materials."[282] Banks had confirmation when he saw wagons—many of them being driven by contraband slaves—headed for the bridge. At the sight of Confederate soldiers in Newtown, many of the African American teamsters panicked that if they were captured they would be murdered by Jackson's men. While some Union soldiers looked upon this behavior as cowardly, others sympathized with their plight. A New York soldier understood their anxieties: "They…knew that they had everything to lose in being captured. There was some excuse for them to act as they did."[283]

With a potential attack, Colonel Dudley Donnelly's brigade deployed to meet the threat. Donnelly's regiments "advanced rapidly" through Middletown and met five companies of Confederate cavalry. With artillery support, Donnelly's brigade drove the Confederates into the fields east of the Valley Pike and pushed them two miles, allowing Banks to place his column on the road once again to Winchester.[284]

Although the Confederate cavalry had not been able to halt Banks's column at Newtown or aggressively engage Donnelly's brigade, it did confirm Banks's withdrawal to Jackson. The Confederate commander hastened his troops along the Old Chapel Road; unfortunately, by the time the head of Jackson's column reached Middletown at about 2:30 p.m., only the rear guard of Banks's army remained. When General John P. Hatch—commanding the Union cavalry rear guard—spied Ashby's troopers entering Middletown, he ordered his men to seek cover. As additional Confederate troops entered Middletown that afternoon, anxieties among the Union troops left behind increased, while the spirits of Middletown's Confederate civilians soared. "Everything in Middletown turned out to greet us," noted Confederate soldier Robert Barton, "men, women, girls, children, dogs, cats, and chickens."[285]

With the Confederate presence increasing, General Hatch turned to Lieutenant Colonel Calvin Douty of the 1st Maine Cavalry and stated simply, "We must cut our way through."[286] Hatch's command lined up four abreast across the Valley Pike and charged north through Middletown. The Union horsemen initially only met fire from the Louisiana soldiers of General Richard Taylor's brigade but suffered a terrible fate when Ashby's cavalry charged into their ranks. To make a bad situation even worse for the Federals, guns from Captain R. Preston Chew's and Captain William Poague's artillery opened fire and inflicted devastation on the Union troopers. "Soon the road was so blockaded with dead men and horses that those in the rear could not pass," recalled a member of Ashby's command of the scene on Middletown's northern edge, "and an indescribable scene of carnage and confusion ensued."[287]

Additionally, Hatch's men were slowed by wagons in his front that had gotten a late start out of Strasburg. This, coupled with the Valley Pike's walls, created a deadly juggernaut. For Confederate artillerists, it became easy target practice that produced results even repulsive to some Confederates. Stonewall Jackson described it as "a most appalling spectacle of carnage and destruction." Eventually, the survivors from Hatch's command either retreated south into Middletown or into the fields west of the Valley Pike, where two years later the Confederates would make their final stand at the Battle of Cedar Creek.[288] Some of Hatch's men who went into Middletown sought refuge in the small white home of Caroline

Ashby's charge at Middletown, May 24, 1862. *From* A History of the Laurel Brigade, *1907.*

Heater, a Unionist sympathizer. "At the time of Banks' retreat," Heater explained, "I secreted some Union men and gave them provisions and sent them on to Winchester."[289]

While Hatch's cavalry succumbed to the Confederate onslaught, Abert and Collis still stood near the Cedar Creek bridge awaiting orders to fire it. Collis could clearly see the troopers' fate and now knew that he was cut off from the main body of Banks's army.[290] Collis also saw the 9th Louisiana marching down Main Street. Like Hatch, Collis realized that he would have to attempt to fight his way out of Middletown. Collis moved his small command—about 150 men—to the cover of a stone wall on the east side of the Valley Pike, south of the village. There Collis's Zouaves d'Afrique delivered well-aimed volleys into their Louisiana counterparts. The Louisianans returned fire and "gave the Zouaves a volley which made their stone breastworks literally shake."[291] Collis soon abandoned his position and fell back to Hupp's Hill, just north of Strasburg.[292] As Collis's command headed south, Abert finally set fire to the bridge. The Confederates halted their pursuit at Cedar Creek and turned north to focus on Banks's main force, which had escaped to Winchester.

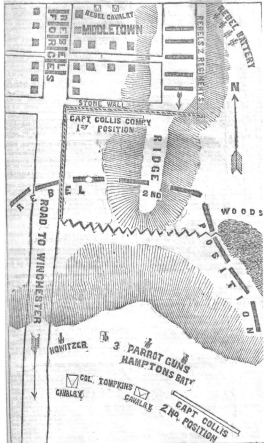

Map of the fight of Collis's Zouaves d'Afrique at Middletown as depicted in the May 31, 1862 edition of the *Philadelphia Inquirer*. *Courtesy of the author.*

As Banks's men arrived in Winchester, the optimism of the town's Confederate population soared, as they believed that Jackson's army was near. "There is every prospect that another battle will be fought tomorrow…We have had a most exciting and fatiguing day," noted the staunch Confederate Laura Lee, "and I feel worn out. We go to bed with the prospect of being roused at daylight by the sound of battle."[293] Optimism, however, among Unionist sympathizers and African Americans was nonexistent. "The Union people are rather uneasy," noted Unionist Julia Chase.[294] African Americans who remained in Winchester held tremendous fears that if they fell into Jackson's hands they would be murdered and that his men were "even cutting the throats of the babies in their cradles." While not all African Americans evacuated Winchester on May 24, untold numbers decided to leave along with a throng of Unionist sympathizers. "Crowds have gone from here today," noted a Winchester resident, "not only runaways, but many who have always been free. There has been a great stampede too among the Union men."[295]

While some civilians took measures for personal safety, Banks gathered his commanders to determine the Union army's next move. He decided to remain and fight. Aware of his numerical inferiority, Banks never fathomed that he would defeat Jackson at Winchester; however, he viewed it as a delaying action that would allow him enough time to move his wagon trains safely across the Potomac. Banks further believed that he needed to keep his army intact so as to block any Confederate threat against the capital. To slow Jackson's advance, Banks arrayed his army in position on Winchester's southern outskirts. He placed Abram's Creek (also known as Abraham's Creek) between his army and the Confederates and anchored both of his flanks on high ground—his left flank rested on an eminence known locally as Camp Hill, and his right stood on Bowers Hill.

Despite the advantage of terrain, expectations among Banks and his officer corps remained low, but all understood that Banks needed to offer battle to Jackson. Division commander General Alpheus Williams noted: "It was decided to make a fight as we were, in front of the town…The prospect was gloomy enough. That we should all be prisoners of war I had little doubt, but we could not get way without a show of resistance, both to know the enemy's position and to give our trains a chance to get to the rear."[296] Unionist sympathizers who remained in Winchester also had no delusions for a chance of Union success. Unionist Julia Chase was angered by the War Department's unwillingness to support Banks. Additionally, she held little faith in Banks's abilities as an army commander. "We can't understand why it is the Secretary of War don't allow Banks to be reinforced," Chase penned on the twenty-fourth. "We have no confidence, however, in Gen. B. and only wish a more able Gen. had been put in command of the forces in the Valley."[297]

At 5:40 a.m., Jackson launched his attack. The Confederate army approached Winchester from two roads—Ewell advanced with a portion of the army on the Front Royal Road to strike Winchester and Banks's left from the southeast, while Jackson took the remainder of the army on the Valley Pike aimed at Banks's right flank. Ewell prepared to strike first at the Federals posted near Camp Hill. He opened his assault with artillery. A soldier in Colonel Dudley Donnelly's brigade, the command responsible for the defense of Camp Hill, noted: "Simultaneously with the starting

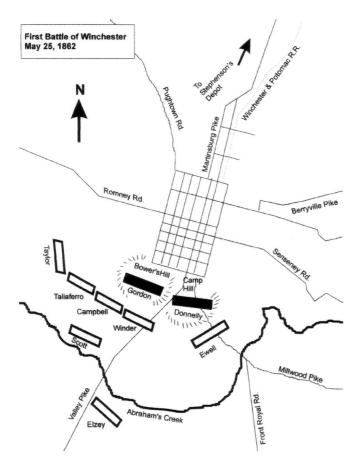

Map of the First Battle of Winchester. *Courtesy of the author.*

of the train the rebels commenced throwing shot and shell."[298] When the battle began, some civilians rushed to catch a glimpse of the action—which through a heavy early morning fog proved impossible—while other civilians used the battle's opening salvos as a final warning to flee. Soldiers in Donnelly's brigade noted that at the first sound of battle they caught sight of an African American woman and several children who made a dash to get out of Winchester. According to a soldier in the 5th Connecticut, however, the woman and her children did not make it and fell victim to a Confederate artillery shell. "She was doing the best she could for freedom and the North," noted a Connecticut veteran, "but when the rebel battery opened up the first shell struck her, and the whole family, bundles and all, disappeared."[299]

After the artillery fired several rounds, "the fog became so dense as to obscure...the town," and Ewell had no alternative other than to capture the Union position with infantry.[300] To lead the assault, Ewell turned to General Isaac Trimble's brigade. Trimble opened the attack with the 21st North Carolina and 21st Georgia—regiments that Trimble affectionately called his "Two 21's."[301] The 21st North Carolina, which in the estimation of one Union soldier "were almost destitute, and looked much like an organization of ragamuffins," along with the 21st Georgia opened fire first on Donnelly's men.[302] The 28th New York and 46th Pennsylvania replied with volleys; however, they did so not to merely defend their position but rather to lure the Confederates closer. Trimble's "Two 21's" had no idea that concealed in a hollow below the New Yorkers and Pennsylvanians lay the 5th Connecticut Infantry.[303]

A Connecticut veteran recalled of their position in the hollow: "Here we dropped out of sight and were entirely concealed by the hollow and standing grain which at that season of the year was pretty full grown."[304] When the Federals spied the Confederate battle standards, "guns and broad-brimmed hats through the grain," the regiment rose and delivered a destructive fire into the North Carolinians and Georgians. "As we rose up, almost a half mile of butternuts stood way back in a solid mass almost squarely with their flanks towards us. It did not seem as if a single bullet of ours," recalled a Connecticut veteran, "let off into that line, could fail to hit somebody."[305] A soldier in the 28th New York who watched the spectacle unfold recorded: "The 5th Conn...arose and poured a volley with deadly effect."[306]

Soon the other regiments of Donnelly's brigade unleashed volleys on Trimble's two lead regiments. As Trimble's troops tried to maintain their organization, the Federals advanced on the Confederate position. The 46th

Pennsylvania, according to one observer, fixed bayonets and surged toward the enemy position. "Bayonets were then fixed, and a charge being made, the traitors were driven from behind a stone wall, where they had taken shelter." For at least the next thirty minutes, the two sides exchanged volleys in a "severe" and "desperate" fight.[307]

Trimble's "Two 21's" clearly needed support from the other regiments in the brigade—the 15th Alabama and 16th Mississippi. The problem, however, was that neither was in a position to offer immediate support. Ewell's attack stalled and the fight became a stalemate. With Donnelly's stout defense of Camp Hill, Jackson needed to focus his efforts on the Union right situated atop Bowers Hill.

When the battle opened against Bowers Hill, Jackson initially determined to soften it with three batteries of artillery.[308] Once Confederate artillery got into position, they fired with great rapidity in an effort to dislodge their counterparts. Union marksmen, however, made it difficult for the Confederate gunners. Robert Barton, a native of Winchester who served in the Rockbridge Artillery, noted that Union infantrymen posted behind a stone fence wreaked havoc on the Rockbridge gunners. "We were working our guns as fast as we could load and fire them," Barton recalled. "About equidistant between the enemy's batteries and ours was a heavy stone fence and behind it a line of Federal infantry had been located, whose good shooting was responsible mainly for the killing and wounding of some twenty-five of our men."[309] The Union defenders under Colonel George Gordon added to the Confederates' difficulties as he moved elements of his command farther to Jackson's left in an effort to flank the Confederate artillery. Regardless of the desperate situation that confronted these artillerists, they refused to relinquish their position. One Confederate officer recalled that the Rockbridge Artillery "was fighting at a great disadvantage, and already much cut up. Poetic authority asserts that 'Old Virginny never tires,' and the conduct of this battery justified the assertion of the Muses…it continued to hammer away at the crushing fire above."[310]

Regardless of the artillerists' tenacity, after about one hour of battle, Jackson realized that only an infantry attack against the Union position would drive Banks out of Winchester. To perform this task, Jackson turned to the shock troops of his valley army—General Richard Taylor's Louisiana Brigade. Jackson ordered Taylor to move his command to Winchester. While his column marched to the town's southern outskirts, Taylor sought

Artillerist Robert T. Barton, like many men in Jackson's army, fought not only for the Confederacy during the Valley Campaign but also fought for home. *Courtesy of the Winchester-Frederick County Historical Society.*

Jackson. When Taylor found Jackson, the army commander pointed to the ridge and ordered: "You must carry it."[311] Taylor had Jackson's orders but did not yet understand how he would carry them out. After surveying the situation, Taylor deemed that only a flank attack could dislodge the Federals. Following Abram's Creek to the west, Taylor's brigade marched to flank Gordon's line. While Taylor's brigade remained concealed for much of the flank march, there were points when the Federals spied the movement and used the opportunity to lob artillery shells into Taylor's command. "We reached the shallow depression spoken of, where the enemy could depress his guns, and his fire became close and fatal. Many men fell," Taylor explained, "and the whistling of shot and shell occasioned much ducking of heads in the column."[312] These reactions frustrated Taylor. The brigade commander lashed out at his men: "What the h[ell] are you dodging for? If there is any more of it, you will be halted under this fire for an hour."[313] After his rant, Taylor

General Richard Taylor soon became one of Jackson's most dependable subordinates. *From Battles and Leaders.*

felt a hand on his shoulder—it was Jackson, who told Taylor "in a gentle voice, 'I am afraid you are a wicked fellow.'" After Jackson's reproach, he left Taylor to carry out his flank attack.[314]

As Taylor positioned his men and prepared to strike the Union right flank, Gordon peered at his attackers and saw "regiment after regiment of the enemy...moving in good order."[315] With attack imminent, Gordon took immediate steps to secure his right flank held by the 2nd Massachusetts. Gordon ordered the 29th Pennsylvania and 27th Indiana to support the 2nd Massachusetts. While Gordon readjusted his line to meet Taylor's attack, the Federals unleashed their muskets. The fire did little to stymie the Confederate advance. "They were received with a destructive fire of musketry," recorded Colonel Gordon, "poured in from all parts of my line that could reach them...the enemy's lines moved on, but little shaken by our fire."[316] A Confederate who observed Taylor's attack noted that as soon as Taylor's brigade came in sight of Bowers Hill, Union artillery and infantry "poured grape and musketry into Taylor's line...They marched up hill in perfect order."[317]

About halfway up the slopes of Bowers Hill, Taylor gave the order for his men to charge. "This charge of Taylor's," noted a Confederate veteran, "was the grandest I saw during the war. There was all the pomp and circumstance of war about it."[318] As Taylor's line surged toward Gordon's brigade, Jackson ordered additional brigades to strike the Union position. As the Confederate assault moved forward, General Jackson, according to

staff officer Henry Kyd Douglas, "cried out 'Very good! Now let's holler!'…
He raised his old grey cap, his staff took up the cheer, and soon from the
advancing line rose and swelled a deafening roar."[319] Confederates who
fought at the First Battle of Winchester believed that this was the first time
the "Rebel yell" was used in the Shenandoah Valley. "For the first time in the
valley, 'the Rebel yell,'" noted a Confederate in Jackson's army, "that strange
fierce cry which heralded the Southern charge, rang high above the storm of
battle."[320] Heavily outnumbered, Gordon's troops had no other alternative
than to withdraw from their position. "Not another man was available,"
Colonel Gordon lamented, "not a support to be found in the remnant of his
army corps left General Banks. To withdraw was now possible; in another
moment it would have been too late."[321]

After Gordon's line broke, General Alpheus Williams ordered four
companies of the 1st Michigan Cavalry to charge the enemy. Major Charles
Town led the attack. General Taylor directed Lieutenant Colonel Francis
T. Nicholls's 8th Louisiana Infantry to stop Town's cavalry. Nicholls's troops
unleashed one volley that "emptied some saddles" and caused Town to
realize the fruitlessness of pressing the attack. Town ordered his troopers to
withdraw. Although Town's charge did not break the enemy assault, Colonel
Thornton Brodhead believed that it served the purpose of a brief delaying
action. "This movement delayed the enemy full ten minutes," Brodhead
observed three days after the battle, "giving our retreating infantry time
to gain the cover of the town."[322] Once the Union right broke on Bowers
Hill, Donnelly's men on Camp Hill suffered the same fate, as Ewell finally
succeeded in his mission.

With the Union defensive line broken, Banks's soldiers retreated through
the gauntlet of Winchester's streets. Although many of Banks's men
retreated from their position, some Union troops did all they could to slow
the Confederate pursuit. For some Union regiments, such as the 10th Maine,
how they handled the Union retreat from Winchester portended their future
fighting prowess. Known to many Union soldiers prior to the First Battle of
Winchester as "the Bandbox Legion," the 10th Maine, amid a tremendous
rain of Confederate artillery, "stood the fire like heroes; their line of battle
was as perfect as if the regiment was on dress parade, and when they fell back
under orders, their battalion was kept in as good shape as though on drill."[323]

During the retreat through Winchester, some angry Confederate civilians
used this opportunity to vent their frustration at their former occupiers.

After the First Battle of Winchester, numerous reports surfaced that accused Confederate civilians—men and women of all ages—of firing on retreating Union soldiers. "Wherever a Union soldier was seen, there a shot was fired. Not men only, but women used with effect the deadly weapons," reported the *Philadelphia Inquirer* five days after the battle.[324] "Citizens, men and women amused themselves by shooting from doors and windows at our retreating troops," noted a veteran of the 28th New York.[325] The 2nd Massachusetts' Robert Gould Shaw seethed with anger over the conduct of Winchester's civilians two days after the battle. "The inhabitants did their share from the windows—women as well as men," Shaw penned his father. "I hope that town will be destroyed when we go back there."[326] According to a report from a Philadelphia newspaper, one Confederate civilian even targeted General Banks. A soldier in the 46th Pennsylvania, John Clark, apparently spied "a Rebel standing in a doorway" with a double-barreled shotgun aimed at Banks. Clark took quick aim and "killed the assassin."[327]

Other Union soldiers also took measures to protect themselves and their comrades. When soldiers from the 28th New York passed through Winchester, they fired back at the civilians and reportedly killed at least two unidentified women. One New Yorker recorded that a Confederate female ended up being shot thirteen times, while another had been shot several times by veterans of the regiment.[328]

Amid the shots, other Confederate civilians rushed into Winchester's streets, heedless of any danger, to greet Jackson's army as liberators. The sight inspired many Confederates, including Jackson. The day following his victory at Winchester, Jackson wrote to his wife: "I do not remember having ever seen such rejoicing as was manifested by the people of Winchester…The people seemed nearly frantic with joy; indeed it would be almost impossible to describe their manifestations of rejoicing and gratitude."[329] Confederate artillerist Robert Barton saw "the women rush out heedless of the shots and embrace their brothers and friends and all the people with enthusiasm and almost crazy with excitement."[330]

Not all of Winchester's citizens greeted Jackson's troops as liberators and expressed joy. The town's Unionist sympathizers and African Americans fretted at what Jackson's victory meant to their future. As Banks's men escaped through Winchester's streets, several thousand African Americans— both slaves and free blacks—gathered their meager belongings and fled north. "The road was lined all the way with families of free negroes who with a bundle in their hands were leaving all for fear Jackson would get them and kill them," recorded a Union commissary sergeant several days after the battle. "I never saw such a lot of blacks in my life, some think as high as 2 or 3,000 of every age and color."[331] Although untold numbers successfully escaped into the north and made their way to Chambersburg and Carlisle, Pennsylvania, an unidentifiable number did not.[332] Once Confederate soldiers pushed through the throngs of civilians in Winchester's streets to the plains north of Winchester, they caught up with some fleeing African Americans. "As we came down the Martinsburg road we met refugees of the colored persuasion," noted Confederate artillerist George Neese. "Each had a little bundle. They evidently started for the land of sweet freedom and glorious ease, but had cut loose from home a 'leetle' too late to make a success of it. Jackson's men overtook them and started the whole caravan back to Winchester."[333]

While Jackson's infantry pushed Banks's column north toward Stephenson's Depot, Jackson eagerly looked for his cavalry to rush out of Winchester's streets and annihilate Banks. "Never have I seen an opportunity," Jackson explained, "when it was in the power of cavalry to reap a richer harvest of the fruits of victory."[334] The Confederate cavalry, however, did not follow up Banks, and Jackson's opportunity to completely annihilate Banks vanished. Some of Jackson's infantry veterans lambasted Ashby's cavalry for not pursuing as Jackson desired. Captain Samuel Buck remarked plainly: "Had we had a good cavalry force we could have captured Banks' army."[335] The Confederate cavalry did not pursue due to lack of desire, but rather due to the fact that the command was busted up from pillaging Union stores the previous day. Ashby had been unable to effectively reorganize his command in time to pursue Banks. This aggravated some Confederate veterans for decades after the conflict. "A braver soldier than Ashby never lived," wrote a Confederate veteran in 1925, "but he lacked a quality, absolutely essential to a successful officer, discipline."[336] Even though the failure of Ashby's command to pursue could not have sat well with Jackson at the moment, Jackson obviously valued Ashby's leadership, as two days after the battle Jackson promoted Ashby to brigadier general.[337]

With the inability of Ashby's cavalry to pursue, Jackson next turned to General Steuart's 2nd and 6th Virginia Cavalry. Jackson sent his young staff officer Sandie Pendleton to find Steuart and order him to pursue Banks. Steuart had no problem with this; however, he wanted the order to

General Alpheus Williams. *Courtesy of the Library of Congress.*

come not from Pendleton but from General Ewell, his immediate superior commander.[338] This took time, and once Steuart had received the order through Ewell, too many moments had been lost and, with it, the opportunity for complete annihilation of Banks's army.

Although Jackson lost the opportunity to completely destroy Banks's force, he did inflict tremendous damage on the Union force. Banks lost more than two thousand men—the majority of whom became prisoners of war—while Jackson suffered only four hundred casualties. Jackson also captured numerous supplies, including 500,000 rounds of ammunition, more than one hundred cattle and in excess of nine thousand firearms. "But the victory was complete and glorious," observed an officer in the Stonewall Brigade, "even if Jackson's weary and march-worn command had not achieved all that their tireless and indomitable leader thought possible."[339]

While Jackson's army enjoyed their success and Jackson lamented a possible lost opportunity, Banks's command retreated north to Williamsport, Maryland. Regardless of their loss, many soldiers in Banks's small army refused to place blame on their commander for the setback but instead directed their frustration at President Lincoln and Secretary Stanton for making decisions about operations in the valley that placed them in a precarious situation that invited defeat. "I hope it will be understood that it was utterly impossible for Genl. Banks to do anything with his small force," observed Robert Gould Shaw. "Mr. Stanton's work in this valley has been pretty unsuccessful & I hope it will all be put on his shoulders."[340] The chaplain of the 2nd Massachusetts viewed the withdrawal from Winchester "as a masterly movement." The chaplain believed that once the nation learned what happened at Winchester, "General Banks, with his gallant little corps, will take high rank in the esteem and affection of the people."[341] General Alpheus Williams also attacked Lincoln's and Stanton's handling of the situation: "The War Department seemed determined to strip Gen. Banks of his whole command…the 'powers that be' at Washington…did not seem to think we were in danger."[342]

Attitudes in Washington changed once they learned of Jackson's victories at Front Royal and Winchester. Fear for the capital's safety increased, and President Lincoln took immediate measures for its protection. First, Lincoln suspended General McDowell's movement on Richmond from Fredericksburg. Lincoln also informed General McClellan of Banks's situation and told McClellan that he must move immediately with the Army of the Potomac against Richmond or come to the capital's defense. "The enemy is moving North in sufficient force to drive Banks," Lincoln wired McClellan on May 25. "I think the time is near when you must either attack Richmond or give up the job and come to the defence of Washington."[343] Furthermore, Lincoln ordered General Fremont to the valley and General Shields's division back to the valley to destroy Jackson.

Unfortunately for Shields's division, they had just arrived in Fredericksburg from their march from the valley to McDowell's corps when they received Lincoln's order to return to the valley. The ragged, ill-equipped men in Shields's division vented their anger. "I trust that the Recording Angel was too much occupied to make a note of the language used in Shields' division when we learned," remembered an artillerist, "with mingled feelings of rage, and mortification, that we were to return to the Valley by forced marches."[344] After the war, men of Shields's command looked back on that order and saw it as the manifestation of Jackson's diversionary operations in the valley and the death knell for McClellan's campaign against Richmond. One veteran referred to it as a "fatal order" that "neutralized an army of nearly 40,000 men…it gave the rebel cause and capital a new lease on life."[345]

As the strategic benefits of Jackson's victory at Front Royal and Winchester came into focus, jubilation erupted in the Confederate capital. "Richmond yesterday experienced a decided and wholesome feeling of elation and rejoicing…of the glorious successes of General Jackson in the Valley of Virginia," reported the *Richmond Examiner*. "It was earnestly hoped the achievements in the valley might speedily find their counterpart nearer Richmond, in the dispersion of the Yankee hosts that environ the capital of the Confederacy."[346] Four days after Jackson's victory, General Joseph E. Johnston issued General Orders No. 58, which praised Jackson's successes.

Optimism permeated the Confederacy in the immediate days that followed Jackson's victory over Banks. Perhaps Winchester's Mary Greenhow Lee captured the hope felt by many in the Confederacy after First Winchester: "The battle has been fought; the victory won; we are free; our precious soldiers are here, in Winchester, with us all the time, morning, noon, & night." Military circumstances, however, proved that Lee's jubilation was premature.[347]

# Chapter 5

# "LIKE MAD DEMONS"

When General John C. Fremont received Lincoln's directive to move into the Shenandoah Valley and support Banks, he contemplated the larger consequences of the order. Lincoln's order called for Fremont to move "immediately" from Franklin to Harrisonburg and cut off Jackson from his supply base at Staunton.[348] Fremont's staff reminded him that the forty-mile path from Harrisonburg to Staunton spanned rugged, mountainous terrain that would move the army farther from its supply base. Consequently, instead of obeying Lincoln's plan, Fremont opted to march his army north (closer to its supply base at New Creek), supply his army and then strike Jackson.[349]

By May 27, Fremont's army stood at Moorefield. There Fremont decided to inform Lincoln of his location and subsequently his alteration of the president's directive to march to Harrisonburg. Fremont's actions outraged Lincoln. "I see that you are at Moorefield. You were expressly ordered to march to Harrisonburg. What does this mean," Lincoln inquired of his general.[350] General Fremont explained to Lincoln that his army's ragged condition precluded him from carrying out the march to Harrisonburg. "The men had so little to eat that many were weak for want of food," Fremont wrote Lincoln.[351] With Fremont's alteration of plans, Secretary of War Stanton ordered the Mountain Department commander to remain at Moorefield until he received further instructions. Direction came from the War Department on May 29 when it ordered Fremont to move toward Strasburg.[352]

Simultaneously with Fremont's movements, General Shields's division made its way toward the lower Shenandoah Valley. Lincoln hoped now that

General John C. Fremont. *Courtesy of the author.*

the two Union commanders could unite near Strasburg and trap Jackson. Although worn ragged from forced marches, Shields's division closed in on the Shenandoah. On May 30, Shields's lead brigade commanded by Colonel Nathan Kimball marched into Front Royal, much to the dismay of the town's Confederate civilians. Front Royal's Lucy Buck referred to that day as "a baneful day" when the Federal troops "poured in from every direction…The horrible beings poured in from all sides looking all the more so since our eyes had grown accustomed to seeing our dear Southerners…I was really sick of heart."[353] The Confederate soldiers who had garrisoned the town, before Kimball's arrival, attempted to destroy the supplies and the buildings of the railroad depot. While the Confederates succeeded in the latter, Union troops extinguished the flames that threatened to consume the supplies badly needed by Shields's division. "A detachment of infantry was hurried forward to extinguish the flames," noted Colonel Kimball, "who by the most strenuous efforts saved several cars loaded with grain, but the buildings were destroyed."[354]

News of Shields's occupation of Front Royal soon reached Winchester. Confederate sympathizers looked on the news in disbelief and feared another Union occupation. "We felt almost despairing at being left again in the hands of our enemies," remembered Winchester's Laura Lee. "We can scarcely bear to think that our little gleam of liberty is ended. The soldiers seemed so sorry and grieved to leave us."[355] Unionists, on the other hand, anticipated their release from Jackson's presence.

When Jackson received news of Shields's occupation of Front Royal and Fremont's movement toward Strasburg, he had no other alternative than to withdraw from the lower valley. Jackson departed Winchester on May 31, much to the dismay of the Confederate civilians. For Kate Sperry, the day proved somber. "I'm sorely afraid the Yanks will come in on us," Sperry confided to her diary. "If they do, the town is doomed—I wish our men could have occupied this place in safety."[356] The withdrawal from Winchester, however, was easier said than done. When Jackson ordered Winchester's evacuation, his command was not fully concentrated around Winchester. Elements were spread throughout the area, and Jackson needed to collect his army quickly and get south of Strasburg before Fremont and Shields united at Strasburg. As Jackson pulled his men south, he received troubling news: Fremont's army was approaching Strasburg from Wardensville. Until he assembled his army at Strasburg, Jackson needed to prevent Fremont from moving any farther east.[357]

By nightfall of May 31, Jackson's army was concentrated in the direction of Strasburg and prepared for the early morning march south toward Harrisonburg. The following morning, Fremont showed an uncommon aggressiveness as he unleashed his artillery on the Confederates from atop Little North Mountain. Confederate artillery soon answered, and infantry from General Ewell's division began to press Fremont's skirmishers. As the Confederate pressure mounted, Fremont backed off and did not engage Jackson's army.[358]

Fremont's failure now meant that both his army and General Shields's division would have to pursue Jackson. Shields moved south through the Luray Valley, east of Massanutten Mountain, while Fremont pursued Jackson south, up the main part of the Shenandoah Valley. By June 3, Jackson's army had

Winchester resident Kate Sperry. *Courtesy of the Winchester-Frederick County Historical Society.*

General Fremont's headquarters in Mount Jackson during his pursuit of Jackson. *Courtesy of the author.*

crossed the North Fork of the Shenandoah River at Meem's Bottom and rested south of New Market. Once across the river, Ashby's cavalry set fire to the bridge, which further impeded Fremont's pursuit. Under normal circumstances, Fremont's men might have been able to ford the Shenandoah River; however, recent rains swelled the river so that no point could be forded. Fremont's only option was to construct a pontoon bridge. Rainstorms over the next two days exacerbated the difficulties confronted by Fremont's engineers. On June 5, Fremont finally caught a break as the rains stopped and the river's waters receded enough to allow the engineers to safely construct the bridge.[359]

Jackson maintained a keen eye on Fremont's pursuit. However, Jackson had not been able to keep a close watch on General Shields to the east. Jackson now needed to anticipate Shields's movements. Undoubtedly, Jackson believed that at some point Shields and Fremont would unite. Jackson knew that if Shields united with Fremont, he would have to cross the South Fork of the Shenandoah. Jackson also understood that all bridges over the river had been destroyed. With this taken into consideration, Jackson surmised that Shields would enter the valley at one point, where a surviving bridge crossed the North River—a tributary that flowed into the South Fork of the Shenandoah—in the small hamlet of Port Republic. Jackson also knew that if he pulled his own army any farther south, the South River, another tributary of the South Fork of the Shenandoah, would be the only other major water barrier between the two Union armies. Unfortunately for Jackson, this river was shallow enough to allow fording opportunities by either Federal force. Port Republic, therefore, emerged as the keystone of Jackson's plan to divide and conquer. From Port Republic, Jackson could strike at either Union army and prevent Federal unification. Jackson also understood that if the situation went terribly wrong for his command, he could easily escape through Brown's Gap in the Blue Ridge Mountains and avoid catastrophe.[360]

As Jackson put his plan in motion, General Fremont pushed south. By the early afternoon of June 6, Fremont's army marched into Harrisonburg. The town's Confederate sympathizers seethed with anger over the presence of Fremont's troops, particularly after Union cavalry rode into town and carelessly fired shots that wounded Harrisonburg resident William Gay. "The Cavelry [sic] came Chargeing [sic] in waving their Swords and whooping…on entering the Town they fired and shot William Gay…just above the hip."[361]

The town's African Americans, however, felt joy at the sight of Fremont's army. Both slaves and free blacks exhibited, in the estimation of one newspaper correspondent, "unmistakable signs of pleasure at seeing the National troops coming round."[362] As had been the case in the lower valley during Banks's occupation, African Americans in the upper valley viewed the Union soldiers as agents of freedom. One Union soldier noticed an African American woman standing outside near a white fence. He called out to her, "What do you think of this gal?" Amid the sound of a marching army, the soldier could not hear her words but noted that "amid the din and rush of martial sounds, [she]…clapped her hands and threw them up in an attitude of glory, hallelujah."[363]

While Fremont's army marched into Harrisonburg, he ordered a cavalry contingent commanded by Colonel Sir Percy Wyndham to reconnoiter south of town. As the troopers rode to the south, Wyndham ordered a charge. Immediately General Ashby countered Wyndham's attack, and according to a chaplain in Ashby's command, the Confederate cavalier "hurled his squadrons with such force and dexterity upon the line of the enemy as to sweep everything before them. The tide of attack was almost instantly met, stemmed, and reversed."[364] During the fight, Ashby's men captured the colors of the 1st New Jersey Cavalry and its commander, Colonel Wyndham.[365]

Following Ashby's successful defense, Fremont's anxieties soared about the potential of a Confederate advance from the east. To prevent this, Fremont ordered troops from General George Bayard's command to block a potential Confederate attack. As Bayard's men got into position, Colonel Thomas

Kane, who commanded the Pennsylvania Bucktails (a contingent of crack riflemen), requested that his men be allowed to go out and collect the dead and wounded Union soldiers from the earlier fight between Wyndham and Ashby. When Ashby saw the Federals advance, he attempted again to counter the impending threat.

Ashby guided the 1st Maryland Infantry and the 58th Virginia Infantry toward the position held by Kane's Bucktails atop a piece of high ground known locally as Chestnut Ridge. General Ashby encouraged the Virginians on horseback; however, once a bullet struck his steed, he urged the Virginians forward on foot. According to one observer, Ashby took no more than six steps and was then shot and killed. "Springing to his feet, and waving his sword over his head, he rushed forward," noted a veteran. "He had not taken half a dozen steps, when he fell, pierced through the body…and died almost instantly…the last command he was heard to give was, 'Forward, my brave men!'"[366] After Ashby fell, the 1st Maryland struck Kane's Bucktails and drove them from their position. Kane suffered a wound in the fight and was captured.

Despite the victory, soldiers in Jackson's command lamented Ashby's death. "Bronzed and scarred veterans, who perhaps for years had not known what it was to shed a tear, wept like children," recorded one veteran.[367] Despite the differences he had with Ashby, Jackson also felt a tremendous sense of loss. "As a partisan officer, I never knew his superior. His daring was proverbial," Jackson explained, "his powers of endurance almost incredible,

Charge of the 1st Maryland at the death of General Turner Ashby on Chestnut Ridge. *From Battles and Leaders.*

his tone of character heroic, and his sagacity almost intuitive of divining the purposes of the enemy."[368] When Jackson visited Ashby's body during the night of June 6 at the Kemper House in Port Republic—where it was cleaned in preparation for its journey and interment in Charlottesville— Jackson "remained for some time in silent communion with the dead."[369]

For valley residents, Ashby became the war's first tragic hero in the Confederacy's Breadbasket. In the aftermath of Ashby's death, citizens from the area journeyed to Port Republic to pay their respects, while others took measures to mark the spot on Chestnut Ridge where Ashby fell by piling stones. For some locales in the valley—including Winchester, where Ashby's remains were moved in October 1866—the date of his death marks the observance of Confederate Memorial Day. Thirty-six years after Ashby's death, on June 6, 1898, veterans gathered on Chestnut Ridge to dedicate

"a simple, but massive block of unpolished Virginia granite" to Ashby's gallantry. Colonel D.H. Lee, who commanded the 10th Virginia Infantry during the war, delivered the dedicatory remarks. The program concluded with a rousing version of "Dixie" and, according to a reporter from the *Baltimore Sun*, "the famous 'rebel yell.'"[370]

The day after the fight at Chestnut Ridge, General Fremont ordered General Milroy's brigade on a reconnaissance toward Port Republic. When Milroy neared the small hamlet of Cross Keys— located about halfway between Harrisonburg and Port Republic—he found

Monument to Turner Ashby on Chestnut Ridge, dedicated on June 6, 1898. *Photo by author.*

Confederate troops from General Ewell's division. Despite some minor skirmishing with his advance guard, Milroy restrained himself and did not attack as Fremont had directed. "I found that they were encamped a short distance…but being positively prohibited by Fremont from bringing on a battle and ordered by him to return I did so reluctantly," Milroy explained to his wife.[371] Milroy's reconnaissance provided Fremont with a valuable piece of information: Jackson was no longer in retreat and he aimed to fight.

The following morning "dawned with all the peaceful brightness appropriate to the Christian's sacred rest," recorded Reverend Robert L. Dabney, one of Jackson's staff. Although Jackson might have preferred to spend this Sunday "in devotion" to God, Federal troops from Shields's command—a detachment commanded by Colonel Samuel Carroll—had other plans.[372] At about 9:00 a.m., Union artillery shredded the morning silence. The sound of enemy artillery compelled Jackson and his staff to mount their horses quickly and escape harm's way. With Jackson's headquarters at Madison Hall on the south side of the North River and his army on the other side, Jackson risked capture. Jackson dashed through the Main Street of Port Republic and across the North River Bridge. Once across the bridge, Jackson saw an artillery piece in Port Republic aimed at the Confederate positions on the North River's northern bank. Jackson ordered his Confederate artillery to fire on it, but they refused on the belief that it was a Confederate gun. Now Jackson seemed uncertain about the artillery crew's identity. Jackson then gestured to the gunners to bring the piece across the bridge. For a moment, the Federal gunners seemed perplexed at their enemy's request, but they soon prepared to fire. As they elevated the barrel, Jackson now knew that it was an enemy cannon. Jackson's artillery opened fire, and Colonel Fulkerson's 37th Virginia charged across the bridge and drove out Carroll's detachment.[373]

While Jackson dealt with Carroll's raid into Port Republic, General Fremont marched his army from Harrisonburg to Cross Keys. Fremont's army marched shortly after 5:00 a.m. More than three hours later, Fremont's advance under General Gustave Paul Cluseret engaged Ewell's advance pickets—two companies of the 15th Alabama—posted north of the Keezletown Road. Colonel James Cantey's Alabamians exchanged fire with Cluseret's pickets but pulled back through the area around the Union Church and toward Ewell's main line. According to an account by one of Cantey's company commanders, Captain William C. Oates, Cantey did not put up much resistance and made a mistake by withdrawing so quickly. "I think, however," Oates wrote after the war, "that he made a mistake in retreating, and should have fought."[374] Others disagreed with Oates's assessment. General Isaac Trimble, Cantey's brigade commander, wrote after the battle of the 15th Alabama: "This regiment was the first engaged, resisting the enemy's advance by a destructive fire from the church, the grave-yard, and the woods."[375] General Fremont also noted that Cantey's Alabamaians "fell back stubbornly through the timber and open grounds."[376] General Ewell likewise discounted Oates's testimony and reported less than two weeks after the battle that the 15th Alabama's resistance was "gallant" and enabled him to place his brigades in "position at leisure."[377]

While Cluseret's and Cantey's men skirmished, Ewell positioned his brigades. General George H. Steuart anchored the left, General Arnold Elzey the center and General Isaac Trimble the right flank. Ewell also placed four artillery batteries to protect the center of the line. Although the position seemed strong to Ewell, General Trimble felt uneasy with his position on the far right flank. Trimble deemed that the heavily wooded condition of the area would not allow him to establish a good defense. Furthermore, Trimble believed that his position bent back from the main line and was "somewhat retired from the front."[378] After he received Ewell's permission, Trimble moved his command forward across the farm of widow Sarah Kiblinger Pence and established his defense in advance of the main Confederate line. Posted on a rise with a split rail fence for cover, Trimble now awaited the Union infantry in his "advantageous" position.[379]

By about 10:00 a.m., Ewell had completed the formation of his line, and Confederate artillerymen unleashed their furious salvos on Fremont's troops near the Keezletown Road. When the guns opened fire, they delivered "their fire with accuracy and spirit."[380] For some in Fremont's command, the accuracy of Ewell's artillery both appalled and astonished. "The diabolical precision with which shot and shell were instantly pitched at us," noted a New York reporter attached to Fremont's army, "exceeded anything I had before imagined. It was as though a platoon of backwoodsmen were firing at us with squirrel rifles—that is, so far as the accuracy of aim and not the size of projectile is concerned."[381]

As Confederate artillery shells rained on Fremont's army, despair increased among civilians whose homes sat near the Keezletown Road. A reporter from the *New York Times* encountered three women and a baby at the Cross

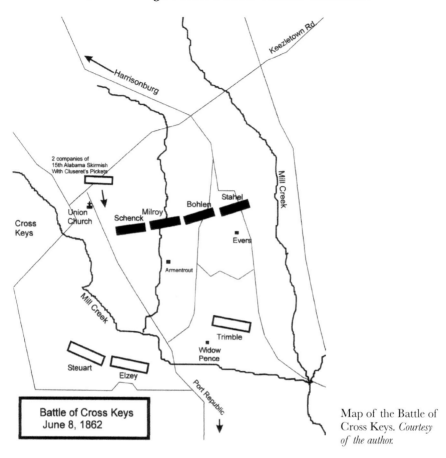

Battle of Cross Keys
June 8, 1862

Map of the Battle of Cross Keys. *Courtesy of the author.*

Keys Tavern "alarmed for their safety." The reporter attempted to quiet their fears and urged them to take shelter; however, the women "locked up the house and departed."[382]

While Fremont's brigades got into position, his artillery chief, Lieutenant Colonel John Pilsen, posted eight artillery batteries within thirty minutes and answered Ewell's guns. Pilsen, noted one of Fremont's staff, concentrated the fire "liberally upon the enemy…pounding away with vigor."[383] Although the Federal artillery fired "with vigor," one of Fremont's brigade commanders, General Milroy, noticed that his three batteries posted near the Armentrout House did not cause any real damage to the Confederate position. Increasingly frustrated with Fremont's lack of aggressiveness throughout much of the campaign, Milroy took it upon himself to move his guns about half a mile beyond the Armentrout House, closer to the Confederate line behind Mill Creek.[384] The Gray Eagle's batteries soon "commenced preaching to the rebels in a most eloquent and striking manner."[385]

While Milroy took matters into his own hands against the left half of Ewell's position, Fremont determined to launch an assault against Ewell's right flank held by Trimble. Fremont believed, despite any accurate military intelligence to reveal this, that Ewell's right flank was his strategic flank. The "Pathfinder" believed that if he could crush Ewell's right, he would also sever Ewell's line of retreat to Port Republic. "I was without reliable maps or guides," Fremont confessed, "but from what could be seen of the roads...I judged the enemy's right flank was his

General Julius Stahel—a native of Hungary—received praise for his heroism at Cross Keys. He received the Medal of Honor in 1893 for heroism at the 1864 Battle of Piedmont. *Courtesy of the author.*

strategic flank. I decided, therefore, to press him from this side, with the object to seize, if possible, his line of retreat."[386]

Fremont launched his initial assault with General Julius Stahel's brigade. The unsuspecting brigade of mainly German immigrants marched forward unaware of their doomed fate. Among Stahel's five regiments, only two actually marched to attack Trimble. With one regiment left behind as battery support and two others having veered off course, only the 8th and 45th New York moved forward to the Confederate position. The 45th New York, however, halted its advance short of Trimble's line. Now the 8th New York stood alone to meet Trimble's men. From their crouched position Trimble ordered his troops "to rest quietly...until the enemy, who were advancing in regular order across the field and hollow, should come within 50 steps of our line."[387] Despite some errant shots from Trimble's men, most adhered

Site of Trimble's defensive line against the 8th New York on the Widow Pence Farm. *Photo by the author.*

to the order, and at close range Trimble opened fire. "A deadly fire was delivered along our whole front…dropping the deluded victims of Northern fanaticism and misrule by scores."[388]

Trimble's men took great comfort in knowing that they had destroyed one of Fremont's "Dutch regiments" made notorious during the valley campaign for the mistreatment of civilians. After the battle, a Richmond newspaper judged that the about 200 casualties suffered out of 548 engaged seemed just retribution for their misconduct. "The Eighth New York Dutch Regiment… were entirely demolished in this action. A just retribution for their excesses in the Valley," wrote the *Richmond Dispatch*, "by insults, robbery, and destruction of property."[389]

Confederates, however, were not the only ones who abhorred the "Dutch" regiments in Fremont's army. Chief among their detractors was General Milroy, who ironically in 1863 returned to the lower valley as an occupation commander and soon came to be regarded as a war criminal by the Confederacy for his brutal treatment of civilians. "The dutch brigades are composed of the most infernal robbers, plunderers, and thieves I have ever seen [and] our army is disgraced by them," Milroy explained to his wife. "Such conduct has injured our cause very much and the…dutch will be celebrated in history as the vandals."[390]

After the 8th New York's destruction, Trimble, who was later referred to as "the anvil at Cross Keys," determined to capture a Union artillery battery to his front.[391] Trimble personally guided the 15th Alabama to a position in the left and rear of the Union line, while the 16th Mississippi and the 21st Georgia advanced against the Union front. As Trimble's regiments advanced, they received support from two Virginia regiments commanded by Colonel James Walker. As the Confederates advanced over the Evers Farm, Union artillery and troops from General Henry Bohlen's brigade greeted them with lead. To a veteran of the 13th Virginia Infantry—one of Walker's regiments— the sight of Bohlen's infantry and artillery raised anxieties tremendously. "We came face to face with more of the enemy than I had ever seen in one position and with several pieces of artillery," recalled the 13th's Samuel Buck, "which opened on us with grape, canister, and small arms which were mowing the wheat about us like a hail storm…most humbly do I now confess, nothing but pride and a sense of duty kept me from running."[392] Despite the perceived strength of the Union position, the Union artillery withdrew after several rounds, north toward the Keezletown Road. Bohlen's brigade soon followed suit.

The incessant pressure placed on the Union left forced Fremont to order a withdrawal of his entire line. Fremont's couriers rode out to the various brigade commanders and issued the general's directive. When General Milroy received word of Fremont's decision, the Indiana general's temper flared. Throughout the day, Milroy's brigade inched its way through a series of ravines toward the Confederate line defended by Steuart's and Elzey's regiments. At the moment when Milroy sent the 25th Ohio on a maneuver against the Confederate left flank, Fremont's courier delivered the order for retreat. Milroy could not believe the instruction and requested that the frightened "Dutchman" repeat it three times. Each time the courier delivered the same message as "balls were whizzing around him like bees and he was dodging his head down behind his horse like a duck dodging thunder."[393] Feeling "ashamed," Milroy reluctantly ordered his brigade to pull out of its position.

Milroy directed his regimental commanders to make the retreat orderly and exert all efforts to collect all of the brigade's dead and wounded before they left the field. As his men tended to that request, Milroy sought out his horse Jasper, his trusted steed since the war's beginning. During the course of the fight, Jasper had received two bullet wounds—one to his leg and the other to his breast. Milroy believed that his horse was dead; however, much to his surprise, he discovered Jasper and guided the animal to the rear on its three good legs. Eventually, Milroy sent the horse home to the care of his wife in Rensselaer, Indiana.[394]

When Milroy returned to the rear, he sought out Fremont. Milroy wanted an explanation as to why Fremont ordered the withdrawal. Milroy recorded that Fremont pleaded ignorance to Milroy's potential success against the Confederate left. "He expressed surprise and said he was sorry he did not know it," Milroy groaned to his wife of Fremont's response. "He has a whole cloud of aids and it was his duty to know everything that was going on [with] his army when in battle."[395] Milroy certainly believed that Fremont abandoned an excellent opportunity at Cross Keys, but he was not alone in his criticism. A reporter attached to the Union army noted that Milroy's attacks against the left half of the Confederate line "if bolstered with an additional regiment or two, would have broken his centre and taken at least one battery."[396] Fremont's apparent lack of leadership and battlefield oblivion, plainly exhibited at Cross Keys, caused tremendous rage among some in his army. "I am thoroughly disgusted with this department," noted one Federal officer. "Fremont is a rabble."[397]

In December 1865, Fremont submitted his official report of his involvement at Cross Keys and attempted to portray his decisions more positively and not reveal any lack of knowledge about Milroy's movements. "Notwithstanding the fair promise held out to an effort on the right," Fremont explained in late 1865, "I judged it best at this point to re-establish my whole line… preparatory to a renewal of the battle."[398] The battle would not be renewed.

As darkness descended over the battlefield, both armies returned to their original lines and counted the battle's cost. Fremont suffered nearly seven hundred casualties, while Ewell suffered slightly fewer than three hundred casualties.[399] The once pastoral scene of these Shenandoah Valley farms was now covered with war's carnage. A reporter for the *New York Times* walked the battlefield and lamented the horrible sight, particularly the portion at which the 8th New York met its slaughter. "The poor fellows lie around in all postures, some on the very spot where they fell, others propped up against the fences where they crawled to die," recorded the New York newspaperman. "Many of them lie on their backs with their arms stretched wearily, carelessly out, in the attitude of men who have thrown themselves on the ground to rest and suddenly sunk into slumber."[400]

Reports circulated that evening of Confederate brutality toward wounded Union soldiers. One Union soldier reported that some Confederates "came down and teased them [the wounded] all night long, taking away their canteens and rifling their pockets." Other stories discounted the reports and illustrated man's capacity to exhibit humanity in times of great personal crisis. During the night of June 8, some Confederates covered wounded Union soldiers with blankets, "brought them water, and in some cases washed their wounds." Actions such as these dispelled the perception, at least in the mind of a reporter for the *New York Times*, that Confederates were nothing but brutal creatures. "What I have here witnessed," the New Yorker explained, "entirely dispels any faint faith I ever had in what is commonly termed 'rebel barbarity.'"[401]

In the Confederate lines that evening, General Trimble looked across the field at the flickering fires of his foe and believed that he had an opportunity to crush Fremont's army by launching a surprise night attack. "I waited in suspense until after dark, saw the enemy go into camp, light their fires, draw rations," Trimble explained, "and otherwise dispose themselves for the night, evidently not expecting any further attack."[402] Trimble sought Ewell's permission; however, he could not find Ewell. When Trimble learned that Ewell left Cross Keys for Jackson's headquarters in Port Republic, Trimble "was strongly tempted to make the advance alone at night."[403] Better judgment prevailed, and Trimble sought the approval of his superior. When Ewell returned to Cross Keys, Trimble urged a night attack. Ewell, however, refused to give the order without General Jackson's consent. Confident in his plan, Trimble rode to Jackson's headquarters. Jackson put the decision in Ewell's hands. When Trimble arrived back in Cross Keys, he sought Ewell's permission, but Ewell now refused to launch a night assault. "You have done well enough for one day," Ewell informed Trimble. Although unable to launch his night attack, Trimble's tenacity at Cross Keys solidified his reputation as a hard-nosed fighter. "No officer of the army has gained suddenly more distinction than Gen. Trimble has done," editorialized the *Richmond Daily Dispatch* after Cross Keys, "by his quick perceptions and swift movements, showing the highest qualities to command."[404]

Ewell did not refuse Trimble's plan due to a lack of personal desire to crush Fremont's army. He denied the request because it might interfere with Jackson's overall plan for the following day. General Ewell knew—from his meeting with Jackson—that Jackson wanted to concentrate his army at Port Republic and strike the Federals there first the following morning. If Confederate success could be achieved quickly at Port Republic, then Jackson would turn his entire army on Fremont. Ewell counseled Trimble that even a partial reverse during a night assault on June 8 "would interfere with General Jackson's plans for the next day."[405]

During the early hours of June 9, Ewell's division marched to Port Republic to carry out Jackson's plan to divide and conquer. As Ewell marched toward Port Republic, he kept a small portion of his command at Cross Keys—including Trimble's brigade—to keep a close eye on Fremont and prevent, or at the very least delay, his efforts to support the Federals at Port Republic. While Ewell's men marched toward Port Republic, Jackson put his plan in motion.

At about 5:00 a.m., General Winder's Stonewall Brigade marched out of its camps, crossed the South Fork of the Shenandoah River on a temporary bridge made of wagons and then marched northeast to strike the Union line, which ran parallel with Lewiston Lane. Although the ground was open in front of Lewiston Lane and presented good fields of fire to the Union defenders, the position took its strength from its flanks. The South Fork of the Shenandoah River guarded the Union right. On the other end of the line—a commanding eminence known as the Coaling—the trees from which were used to produce charcoal for the Lewis family (whose home sat at the hill's base) protected the Federal left.[406] Jackson noted simply of the Union line: "The enemy had judiciously selected his position for defense."[407] The Federals needed every advantage they could muster at Port Republic. Shields had not been able to concentrate his entire force. Even he had not been able to make it to Port Republic in time to direct his troops in battle. That responsibility fell upon one of his brigade commanders, General Erastus B. Tyler. By the morning of June 9, Tyler commanded a force of about four thousand Federals, which consisted of two infantry brigades and three artillery batteries.

As Winder advanced toward Tyler's line, he divided his brigade. He first sent the 5th and 27th Virginia to attack the Union right flank. Before Winder launched his infantry assault, he intended to soften the Union flank with Captain Poague's artillery. Poague placed two cannons and opened on the Federal line. After a few rounds, Union artillery pinpointed Poague's guns and fired on them with precision. For at least one hour, by some accounts, the artillery of both sides dueled.[408] The accuracy of the Union artillery prompted Winder to separate Poague's two guns. Clearly the Union artillery held the advantage at Port Republic. "The artillery fire was well sustained by our batteries," Stonewall Jackson observed, "but found unequal to that of the enemy."[409]

During the artillery duel, Winder hoped that Poague's guns would not only weaken the Union line but that it would also allow time for reinforcements to arrive in support of the infantry assault. Due to circumstances beyond Winder's control, however, Jackson had a difficult time getting support to Winder. Chaos reigned in Port Republic's streets as they became clogged with army wagons. Only one regiment initially could be sent to Winder's aid, the 7th Louisiana. Time concerned Jackson at this point. Before the battle began, Jackson hoped that he would be able to crush the Federals at Port Republic by 10:00 a.m. and then turn to the northwest to destroy Fremont. If Jackson had any hope of crushing both Shields and Fremont, Winder needed to attack immediately without proper support.[410]

With the 5th Virginia on the left, the 7th Louisiana in the center and the 27th Virginia on the right, the Confederates moved toward Lewiston Lane. As the Confederates closed in on Union pickets, the regimental officers readied their men. The 29th Ohio's regimental commander, Colonel Lewis Buckley, ordered his men to "aim low…and at every shot let a traitor fall!"[411] When the Confederates neared the Federal position, the Union line belched forth furious volleys. "When in close range the rebels charged," recalled a member of the 29th Ohio. "Reserving our fire until they were almost upon us, the order was given, and with a yell the entire line poured its leaden hail into the gray clad columns of the chivalry, producing fearful slaughter."[412] A veteran of the 7th Ohio noted simply: "This shower of lead made a fearful gap in the lines of the advancing column. It staggered, and finally halted."[413]

Despite Winder's best efforts, his partial command could not break the Union right. As the Confederates relinquished their ground, troops from Carroll's brigade left their lines and attacked the Confederates "with a charge so impetuous that they were forced to retire."[414] "The Federalists now advanced from their cover," recorded a member of Jackson's staff, "with loud and taunting cheers, pierced the center of Jackson's feeble line, and threatened to throw the fugitives against the river."[415] As the Federals charged, Poague's gunners went to limber the guns; however, only one gun could be removed from the field. When the crew of the second gun went to

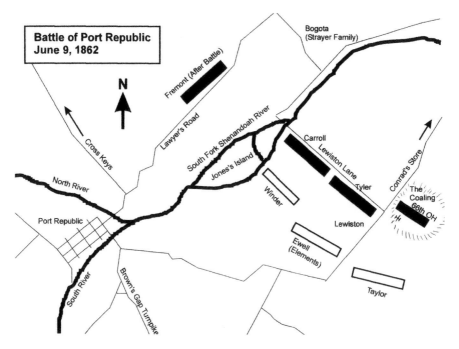

Map of the Battle of Port Republic. *Courtesy of the author.*

limber the piece, they discovered that all of the horses had been killed. As a result, Poague ordered the gun to remain on the field as long as possible and then abandon it in favor of personal safety. Robert Barton remembered the closeness of the Federal soldiers before they ceased fire and abandoned the gun: "We could almost tell the colors of the eyes of the enemy before we were ordered to cease firing and fall back."[416]

Although two Virginia regiments—the 44th and 58th Virginia—arrived on the field to support Winder and prompted the Federals to stop their attack and return to their line along Lewiston Lane, Stonewall Jackson fully realized that the key to Confederate success was the Coaling.[417] Jackson also realized that he would not meet his objective of driving the Federals by 10:00 a.m., and therefore he abandoned any hope of crushing Fremont that day.

Jackson now focused his efforts on the Union left flank and the artillery ensconced atop the heights. Initial assaults against the position proved that it would be no easy task to drive the guns from portions of Huntington's, Robinson's and Clark's Batteries off the commanding eminence. During the opening Confederate attack, Winder sent the other half of his command against the position. The 2nd and 4th Virginia, along with a two-gun section of artillery from Carpenter's Battery, moved to strike. Union gunners atop the Coaling, along with their scant infantry support, delivered volleys into the attacking Confederates that destroyed this portion of Winder's advance and sent them rearward. One Confederate officer noted that the Virginia troops who initially attempted to attack the Coaling were "subjected to a heavy fire of musketry and canister…thrown into confusion and forced to retire."[418]

With the Virginia regiments unable to achieve any success, Jackson turned to the shock troops of his valley army, General Taylor's brigade. They won the day for him at Winchester, and now would be asked to do the same at Port Republic. According to General Taylor's postwar writings, he had a conversation with Jackson about the particulars of the attack; however, other accounts state that Jackson had no conversation with Taylor. Recent scholarship on Port Republic states that Jackson relayed his desire for Taylor's brigade to attack the Coaling through cartographer Jed Hotchkiss. "Take Gen. Taylor around and take those batteries," Hotchkiss penned of the encounter in his wartime journal.[419] Regardless of how Taylor received the order, his soldiers greeted their mission with enthusiasm. Taylor shouted above the din of battle and asked his men if they could take the Union position. "The answer was a Rebel yell," remembered one Confederate veteran, "and three hundred and eighty Louisianans, rushed to the top of that hill."[420]

As Taylor's men assaulted the Coaling, Union gunners loaded whatever they could into the cannon. "During this hot conflict the gunners fired grape," noted a Union veteran, "chains and even the rat-tail files supplied to each battery for spiking guns."[421] An artillerist who defended the Coaling wrote that the Union artillery gave the Confederate attackers "canister in allopathic doses."[422] Confederate soldiers who observed Taylor's attack seemed awe-inspired by the scene. "I saw General Dick Taylor's Louisianans debouching from the undergrowth, and like a wave crested with shining steel rush toward the fatal coaling and deadly battery with fixed bayonets," remembered a Confederate artilleryman, "giving the Rebel yell like mad demons."[423]

Taylor's first two assaults were repulsed after severe hand-to-hand combat. During the assaults, one of Taylor's regimental officers, Major Chatham Roberdeau Wheat, used his knife to cut the throats of the Union horses so that the Federals would not be able to evacuate the guns. Wheat, recalled one Confederate, "was as bloody as a butcher."[424] Union gunners and infantry support from the 66th Ohio defended their position tenaciously. The infantry used bayonets and clubbed muskets, while the gunners defended their pieces with "their rammers in a way not laid down in the Manual…Twas claw for claw" recalled General Taylor.[425]

Mounting casualties, however, and the weight of Taylor's third assault, along with the presence of additional reinforcements from General Ewell, gave the Federals no other alternative but to surrender their position.[426] "The Federals held to the coaling with bulldog tenacity…as it was the citadel of strength in Shields's line and the key to his position," remembered one Confederate veteran, "but the firm and unwavering courage and invincible prowess of Taylor's Louisianans made them as persistent and obdurate, in gaining and demanding, at the point of the bayonet, full possession and control of the death shelf."[427] Once the Coaling fell to Taylor, the remainder of the Union line withdrew. Jackson had achieved another victory. It did not come without cost. Each side suffered about one thousand casualties. Losses among the Coaling's defenders proved appalling. For example, of the eighty members of the 66th Ohio's Company A, only six survived the fight.[428] Confederates who walked around the hotly contested spot after the battle recorded the gruesome scene. "It was a sickening sight," noted a veteran of the 13th Virginia. "Men in grey and those in blue piled up in front of and around the guns and with horses dying and the blood of men and beasts flowing almost in a stream."[429]

By about 11:00 a.m., Jackson secured victory at Port Republic. Elements of Jackson's army, including infantry and cavalry, pursued Tyler's battered Union force for about eight miles and then returned to Port Republic. As the Federals abandoned their positions, General Fremont's army finally arrived. However, the South Fork of the Shenandoah River prevented him from offering any real support to the retreating Federals. Fremont unlimbered his guns on the north bank of the river and displayed his anger toward the Confederates by firing on ambulances and men as they policed the battlefield. "His…rage was so great that his artillery was turned upon our ambulances," recalled Alabamian William Oates, "and parties engaged in the humane labors of attending to the dead and wounded of both sides."[430] "There were several burying parties…sacrilegiously interrupted in their kindly service to the dead by being fired on by some of Fremont's batteries on the hill beyond the river," wrote Confederate George Neese, "an act in itself so atrocious that it would make even a barbarous vandal blush with shame to be guilty of its perpetration."[431]

Some of Fremont's men also took out their frustration on civilians living on the west bank of the South Fork of the Shenandoah River. Troops from Stahel's and Bohlen's brigades ransacked Bogota, the Strayer home. During the battle, the Strayers and refugees from the other side of the river watched the battle unfold from Bogota. Now the war came to their doorstep. The "Dutch" soldiers entered the house and "stripped it all of edibles," according to Clara Strayer. Although Fremont's men pillaged the property, the Strayer family gained some satisfaction when Union soldiers attempted to steal a beehive and were attacked by a swarm.[432]

In Port Republic's aftermath, soldiers from Shields's command felt dejected and lamented their loss. Some soldiers placed blame variously on Shields, Fremont's inability to provide proper support, interference from Washington, D.C., or Jackson's generalship as the cause of Union defeat not only at Port Republic but throughout the entire valley that spring as well. "Our failure was due to the military skill and boundless audacity of the Confederate leaders, as opposed to…'the presumptuous incapacity of those who directed the operations against Jackson from Washington,'" explained an artillery officer in Shields's command, "to the blundering of Shields and the sluggishness of Fremont."[433] The only redeeming quality for Federals who fought at Port Republic was the tenacity that they displayed in defense of their position against a Confederate force three times their size. "Those engaged in it," noted Union artillerist James Gildea, "pride themselves more on it than on any other battle, even Gettysburg, and the rebel soldiers respect a man who was on the union side more than they do any other."[434] Artillerist James Huntington echoed: "The only redeeming feature of the operation is found in the valor of the troops who did the actual fighting."[435]

After the Confederate success at Port Republic, Jackson's army marched to Brown's Gap—a place in the Blue Ridge that allowed Jackson flexibility to deal with a potential advance by Fremont or Shields. After several days in Brown's Gap, Fremont or Shields made no move to threaten Jackson. Fremont pulled his army back to Harrisonburg and then eventually north, down the valley, while Shields held his command at Luray. Without fear of Federal pursuit, Jackson returned his men to the valley and established camp in the small hamlet of Weyers Cave.

In the aftermath of Confederate victory, Jackson again thanked God for the victory and praised his men. On the thirteenth, he issued a proclamation in honor of his men's tenacity: "Beset on both flanks by two boastful armies, you have escaped their toils, inflicting successively crushing blows upon each of your pursuers. Let a few more such efforts be made and you may confidently hope that our beautiful valley will be cleansed from the pollution of the invader's presence."[436]

Jackson's congratulatory order undoubtedly pleased many in the army, but not all. Some of Jackson's subordinates—including General Winder—seethed with anger after Port Republic over Jackson's tactical management of the battle. Some subordinates believed that Jackson's inability to wait for the army to be concentrated and funneling regiments into the battle piecemeal produced unnecessary casualties. Some of Jackson's lieutenants also felt that Jackson might have worked the men too hard throughout the campaign. Robert Dabney, who served on Jackson's staff and in 1866 published a glowing biography of Jackson, complained to his wife on June 12, 1862, about Jackson pushing the men too hard. "Indeed Jackson's great fault is that he marches and works his men with such disregard to their physical endurance. His victories are as fatal to his own armies as to his enemies. The former he kills," Dabney explained, "the latter he works nearly to death."[437]

Despite his few detractors, Jackson's aggressiveness in the valley achieved significant strategic gains for the Confederacy at a time when all seemed to go badly on every other front. Simply put, Jackson's victories became the lone crutch that supported the militarily beleaguered Confederacy in the first half of 1862.

After victory at Cross Keys and Port Republic, Jackson hoped for reinforcements that would permit him to annihilate the remaining Federal forces in the valley and then cross the Potomac into the North. Circumstances, however, prevented it. The Army of Northern Virginia's new commander, General Robert E. Lee, needed Jackson's men to crush the Army of the Potomac before Richmond. Jackson's strategic diversion paid huge dividends to the Confederacy's operations to protect the capital in the spring, but now Lee believed that Jackson's troops would do greater service east of the Blue Ridge. On June 18, Jackson's army crossed the Blue Ridge and his Valley Campaign officially came to a close. Although the campaign had ended, what Jackson achieved during the spring of 1862, against various obstacles, not only inspired the Confederacy but also solidified Jackson's enduring legacy. Jackson's Valley Campaign had now become, as one British observer explained in 1864, "a chapter in history which is without parallel."[438]

# Chapter 6

# "THIS CAMPAIGN MADE THE FAME OF JACKSON"

Throughout the spring of 1862, many individuals throughout the Confederacy—soldiers and civilians alike—looked to Stonewall Jackson for hope and inspiration. Jackson's strategic ability coupled with the timing of his successes in the valley transformed Jackson from mere general to the Confederacy's lone beacon of optimism.[439]

"This Stonewall—how he fires the soldiers' hearts…He fights to win—God bless him—and he wins," penned South Carolinian Mary Chestnut.[440] The famed wartime diarist even went so far as to suggest that Jackson's successes might catapult him to leadership of the entire Confederacy. "He will be our leader—maybe—after all," Chestnut surmised in June 1862.[441] A civilian in Georgia greeted news of Jackson's success with great enthusiasm and hoped that it might portend future victory on other fronts. "Great and good news from that great and good General Stonewall Jackson," penned Georgia's Charles C. Jones. "The rout has fallen on the right head this time: Banks. May it be the prelude of what the Lord will do for us at Corinth and at Richmond."[442] Judith Brockenbrough McGuire, who at the time of Jackson's Valley Campaign resided in Richmond, noted that the depressing news of Confederate setbacks, particularly the scuttling of the CSS *Virginia*, ought not to demoralize the Confederacy so long as Jackson continued his successes west of the Blue Ridge. "General Jackson is doing so gloriously in the Valley," McGuire wrote, "that we must not let the fate of the 'Virginia' depress us too much."[443]

Soldiers in other theaters of war also looked to Jackson for inspiration and looked to connect themselves with Stonewall Jackson in any way possible, regardless of how far they might have been from the valley. For example, Confederates stationed near James Island, South Carolina, during the second week of June 1862 named their bivouac "Camp Stonewall Jackson."[444] In the estimation of Winchester's Reverend Robert Graham, Jackson "was the hero around whom…the war principally gathered, and in whom the interest of the great masses centered."[445]

Indeed, by the second week of June, Stonewall Jackson's exploits in the valley had buoyed many Confederate spirits. "This campaign made the fame of Jackson as a commander…The rumor of his rapid movements and constant successes came like a wind from the mountains to the Confederate capital," wrote John Esten Cooke after the war, "and infused fresh life into the languid pulses and desponding hearts of the people."[446]

Jackson's exploits in the valley also caught the attention of many in the North, as well. By the time Jackson's valley campaign had ended, the Union feared Jackson as much as the Confederacy admired him. "This most extraordinary man appeared suddenly in the military firmament as a dazzling Meteor," explained Confederate vice-president Alexander Stephens after the war, "or rather as a blazing and fiery Comet, exciting the highest admiration on one side, and causing profound fear and terror on the other."[447]

Despite the fear that Jackson's name might have stirred in the North, some, including the Northern media, admired Jackson's abilities put on display during operations in the Shenandoah Valley. "One thing is certain," penned the *New York Times* one week after the Battle of Port Republic, "Jackson is equally eminent as a strategist and tactician. He handles his army like a whip, making it crack out of the way corners where you scarcely thought the lash would reach."[448] Respect for Jackson's abilities among some Northerners caused at least one Northern company to take advantage of Jackson's image for marketing purposes. Pyles O.K. Soap utilized Stonewall Jackson's popularity to sell its product. The company contended that Jackson did all that he could in the field to seize it and that when he ran out he longed for more.[449]

In the eleven months that followed the campaign in the valley, Jackson served as an integral part of the Army of Northern Virginia's operations. After a somewhat lackluster performance during the Seven Days' Campaign— undoubtedly brought on by utter exhaustion from the Valley Campaign— Jackson performed admirably throughout the remainder of 1862 as commander of Lee's Second Corps.[450] In the spring of 1863, the indomitable team of Lee and Jackson reached its final crescendo at Chancellorsville.

Jackson performed arguably his greatest tactical feat on May 2, 1863, by flanking General Joseph Hooker's Army of the Potomac. Then, at the height of his military stature, Jackson very unfortuitously was struck by friendly fire on the night of that great achievement. Eight days later, Jackson died.

News of Jackson's death sent shockwaves throughout the Confederacy. "The death of our pious, brave, and noble General Stonewall Jackson is a great blow to our cause," lamented a Georgia woman.[451] While sadness hung like a pall over the Confederacy, perhaps no region mourned Jackson's death more than the Shenandoah Valley. After all, Jackson had called the valley home and had a special connection with its Confederates as their first liberator from Union occupation. Winchester's Mary Lee noted sorrowfully that the "idea has given me a more hopeless feeling than any other event of the war. Not that I despair at the final result, but it would be as if God were for awhile leaving us to grope in the dark—in depriving us of one of His purest saints."[452] Valley native Kate Sperry confided to her diary three days after Jackson's death: "I...feel so miserable—nearly cried my eyes out—poor Jackson—so noble—so brave—so loved by all the people—Oh, how we shall miss him...There was no more pleasure for me after that dreadful news."[453]

Some Northerners, too, reacted to Jackson's death with respect. The ardent anti-Confederate Herman Melville penned two poems about Jackson. Although Melville did not agree with the cause for which Jackson fought, he could not refuse to ignore his greatness as a general.[454] Admiration along the same lines as Melville even made it into President Lincoln's staff. "Jackson was by far the most interesting and picturesque figures in the Southern army. His brilliant successes and his early death," wrote one of Lincoln's personal secretaries, "enshrined him in the hearts of his associates as their foremost champion...it cannot be contested that General Jackson was a man of extraordinary qualities."[455] Even Lincoln, who undoubtedly had many sleepless nights because of Jackson's exploits in the valley, showed respect for Jackson after his death. When a Washington newspaper, the *Chronicle*, published an editorial about Jackson that celebrated the Confederate general's attributes, President Lincoln sent a note to the paper that thanked it "for the excellent and manly article...on 'Stonewall Jackson.'"[456]

In the aftermath of Jackson's death, his popularity again soared, and certain individuals saw an opportunity to capitalize on that fame. Within months after Jackson's death, the London publishing house of Chapman and Hall published Catherine Cooper Hopley's *"Stonewall" Jackson, Late General of the Confederate States Army: A Biographical Sketch, and an Outline of His Virginian Campaigns.* A Southerner, Hopley portrayed Jackson's operations in the valley in glorious terms but did nothing to place the valley campaign in perspective as the defining moment of Jackson's career. Also in 1863, Markenfield Addey, a Northerner who utilized a Northern publishing company, released his admiring biography *"Stonewall Jackson": The Life and Military Career of Thomas Jonathan Jackson, Lieutenant-General in the Confederate Army.*[457]

Throughout his Civil War career, Jackson contributed mightily to the Confederate war effort. He produced many memorable moments; however, every figure throughout the course of history always has one moment— above all others—that defines his legacy. While some might contend that Jackson's defining moment came at the First Battle of Manassas, at which he earned his eternal sobriquet, First Manassas only initiated the legend. The 1862 Valley Campaign solidified his reputation in both the North and South. The Shenandoah Valley Campaign offered the only moment where Jackson's generalship could be put on full display—a generalship still studied at military academies around the world.[458] Confederate artillerist E. Porter Alexander observed of the Valley Campaign as Jackson's defining moment: "Early in June, Gen. Stonewall Jackson, whose reputation up to this time had simply been that of a desperate & stubborn fighter…suddenly broke loose up the Valley of Virginia & not only astonished the…enemy…but dazzled the eyes of military men all over the world by an aggressive campaign which I believe to be unsurpassed in all military history for brilliancy & daring."[459]

Beyond the personal observations of individuals on both sides, artwork produced in the immediate aftermath of Jackson's death also helps solidify the Valley Campaign's role as Jackson's defining moment. Two of the earliest paintings produced after Jackson's death used events from Jackson's Valley Campaign to immortalize the fallen general—an indicator of the campaign's central role in defining Jackson's legacy.

The first painting, produced by Louis M.D. Guillaume, depicted Jackson at the First Battle of Winchester, holding his arm out with hat in hand and urging his men forward as they climbed Bowers Hill. Guillaume, who came to the United States from France in 1855, settled in Richmond by 1857. In the war's aftermath, Guillame was commissioned to paint six portraits, one of which was of Jackson. Of all of Jackson's moments, including his flank attack at Chancellorsville, Guillaume chose First Winchester as the setting for the painting.[460]

Louis M.D. Guillaume's oil painting of Stonewall Jackson at the First Battle of Winchester. *Courtesy of the R.W. Norton Art Gallery, Shreveport, Louisiana.*

The second painting, created by William D. Washington, also utilized Winchester as the setting to immortalize Jackson's legacy. Washington, a native of the Shenandoah Valley who also served in the Confederate army during the war, was (like Guillaume) in Richmond at the time of Jackson's death. Washington depicted a victorious Jackson riding down Winchester's Loudoun Street (the downtown walking mall today), being greeted by joyous Confederate civilians. The valley native's artistic portrayal of Jackson entering Winchester had become by the time of his death in 1870 among his two most popular paintings; the other was his *Burial of Latane.*[461]

If one trusts the validity of artwork as a tool of historical interpretation, as did the nineteenth-century English intellectual John Ruskin, then Guillaume's and Washington's portrayals of Jackson at Winchester might even suggest that within the Valley Campaign's role in defining Jackson's legacy, the First Battle of Winchester became the crucial moment.[462] While historians might wish to debate Jackson's defining moment in the campaign, at least one

William D. Washington's oil painting depicting Stonewall Jackson's entrance into Winchester. *Courtesy of the Valentine Richmond History Center.*

contemporary believed that Winchester became the central moment that catapulted Jackson to fame. "Stonewall Jackson is one of the many men whose extraordinary military genius has been developed by the Civil War," penned Northern journalist George Alfred Townsend. "Jackson's glory has steadily increased. He was first brought into notice at Winchester."[463]

Admiration for Jackson abounded in the aftermath of his death and still persists until this day.[464] While he had a celebrated military career, Jackson's Valley Campaign catapulted him to the pantheon of military legends. As Jackson's widow Mary Anna reflected on her husband's career, she also concluded that his defining moment came in the valley. "Brilliant as were the achievements of General Jackson during the succeeding months of his too brief career," Mary Anna penned, "it was his Valley Campaign which lifted him into great fame; nor do any of his subsequent achievements show more striking the characteristics of his genius."[465]

# NOTES

## INTRODUCTION

1. Trowbridge, *The South*, 69.
2. Shenandoah Valley Battlefields Foundation, *Shenandoah Valley Battlefields*, i.

## CHAPTER 1

3. Julia Chase Diary, March 3, 1862, Julia Chase Collection, Stewart Bell Jr. Archives, Handley Library, Winchester, VA. Items from this repository will hereafter be cited as HL.
4. Robertson Jr., *Stonewall Jackson*, 330–31.
5. Jackson, *Memoirs of Stonewall Jackson*, 239; Robertson Jr., *Stonewall Jackson*, 330.
6. Jackson to Mary Anna, March 17, 1862, quoted in Jackson, *Memoirs of Stonewall Jackson*, 243.
7. Allan, *History of the Campaign*, 41.
8. Ibid.
9. Sperry, *Surrender? Never Surrender!*, March 7, 1862, Kate Sperry Papers, HL.
10. Cozzens, *Shenandoah 1862*, 131.
11. U.S. War Department, comp., *War of the Rebellion*, ser. 1, vol. 5, 738, hereafter cited as *OR*.
12. Ibid., 1094–95.

13. Ibid., 1095.

14. For additional discussion of the circumstances leading to Johnston's withdrawal, see Sears, *To the Gates of Richmond*, 13–15.

15. Johnston, *Narrative of Military Operations*, 106.

16. For additional discussions on the complexities of Unionist sentiment, see Noyalas, *"My Will Is Absolute Law,"* 95–96; Emmert F. Bittinger, "Dissenters from the 'Southern Cause': Unionists in the Shenandoah Valley," in Noyalas, ed., *Home Front to Front Line*, 26–36; Inscoe and Kenzer, eds., *Enemies of the Country*; Berkey, "War in the Borderland," PhD dissertation, Pennsylvania State University, 2003.

17. Cozzens, *Shenandoah 1862*, 133.

18. Julia Chase Diary, March 11, 1862, Julia Chase Collection, HL.

19. Ibid., March 10, 1862.

20. Eby Jr., ed., *A Virginia Yankee in the Civil War*, 14.

21. Graham, "Some Reminiscences of Stonewall Jackson," 95–99.

22. Jackson, *Memoirs of Stonewall Jackson*, 241.

23. Graham, "Some Reminiscences of Stonewall Jackson," 96.

24. Colonel William Allan, "Address of Colonel William Allan on Jackson's Valley Campaign," in Jones, comp., *Army of Northern Virginia Memorial Volume*, 267.

25. Mary Greenhow Lee Diary, March 11, 1862, Mrs. Hugh Lee Collection, HL.

26. Gwin, ed., *A Woman's Civil War*, 23.

27. Mohr, ed., *Magnificent Irishman from Appalachia*, 14.

28. Quaife, ed., *From the Cannon's Mouth*, 62.

29. For a discussion of the reaction of African Americans to Banks's occupation of the lower valley, see Noyalas, *Two Peoples, One Community*, 25–27.

30. Julia Chase Diary, March 12, 1862, Julia Chase Collection, HL.

31. John Peyton Clark Journal, March 12, 1862, Louisa Crawford Collection, HL.

32. Mary Greenhow Lee Diary, March 12, 1862, Mrs. Hugh Lee Collection, HL.

33. Sperry, *Surrender? Never Surrender!*, March 16, 1862, Kate Sperry Papers, HL.

34. Duncan, ed., *Blue-Eyed Child of Fortune*, 182.

35. Quint, *Potomac and Rapidan*, 111.

36. Noyalas, *Plagued by War*, 40–41.

37. John Peyton Clark Journal, March 20, 1862, Louisa Crawford Collection, HL.

38. Noyalas, *Two Peoples, One Community*, 27.

39. Laura Lee Diary, March 14, 1862, Swem Library, College of William and Mary, Williamsburg, Virginia.

40. Sperry, *Surrender? Never Surrender!*, March 17, 1862, Kate Sperry Papers, HL.

41. Berkey, "War in the Borderland," 191.

42. Sears, *To the Gates of Richmond*, 16–17.

43. Nicolay and Hay, eds., *Complete Works of Abraham Lincoln*, 7:129–30.

44. Ibid., 117.

45. Rowland, *George B. McClellan and Civil War History*, 103–4.

46. Nicolay and Hay, eds., *Complete Works of Abraham Lincoln*, 7:117.

47. Cozzens, *Shenandoah 1862*, 148; Sears, ed., *Civil War Papers of George B. McClellan*, 212.

48. Work, *Lincoln's Political Generals*, 22.

49. Johnson, ed., *Battleground Adventures*, 396.

50. *OR*, ser. 1, vol. 12, pt. 1, 6.

51. Testimony of Jacob F. Larrick, Heater Claim on Loyalty, Belle Grove Collection, Box 13, HL.

52. *OR*, ser. 1, vol. 12, pt. 1, 380.

53. Henderson, *Stonewall Jackson*, 179.

54. *OR*, ser. 1, vol. 12, pt. 1, 380.

55. Johnston to Jackson, March 19, 1862, quoted in Ecelbarger, *"We Are In for It!,"* 64.

# CHAPTER 2

56. Robertson Jr., *Stonewall Brigade*, 70.

57. Casler, *Four Years in the Stonewall Brigade*, 64.

58. Neese, *Three Years in the Confederate Horse Artillery*, 31.

59. Ecelbarger, *"We Are In for It!,"* 71.

60. *OR*, ser. 1, vol. 12, pt. 1, 355–56.

61. Avirett, *Memoirs of General Turner Ashby*, 157.

62. *OR*, ser. 1, vol. 12, pt. 1, 339.

63. *Philadelphia Press*, March 28, 1862.

64. Ecelbarger, *"We Are In for It!,"* 71.

65. Neese, *Three Years in the Confederate Horse Artillery*, 32.

66. Ibid.

67. *OR*, ser. 1, vol. 12, pt. 1, 359.

68. Neese, *Three Years in the Confederate Horse Artillery*, 32.

69. SeCheverell, *Journal History of the Twenty-Ninth*, 39.

70. Ibid.

71. Avirett, *Memoirs of General Turner Ashby*, 157.

72. Neese, *Three Years in the Confederate Horse Artillery*, 31.

73. *OR*, ser. 1, vol. 12, pt. 1, 339.

74. McDonald, *History of the Laurel Brigade*, 40.

75. Jackson, *Memoirs of Stonewall Jackson*, 248–49.

76. Ibid., 243.

77. James F. Huntington, "Winchester to Port Republic," in Dwight, *Campaigns in Virginia*, 1:6.

78. Allan, *History of the Campaign*, 44–45; *OR*, ser. 1, vol. 12, pt. 1, 339.

79. *OR*, ser. 1, vol. 12, pt. 1, 339.

80. Allan, *History of the Campaign*, 45.

81. *OR*, ser. 1, vol. 12, pt. 1, 389. Three of the infantry companies (D, H and I) were from the 2nd Virginia Infantry, and one infantry company (H) was from the 27th Virginia Infantry.

82. Ibid., 359.

83. Ibid., 373.

84. Neese, *Three Years in the Confederate Horse Artillery*, 33.

85. Ibid.

86. Ibid.

87. Ibid., 33–34.

88. Johnson and Buel, eds., *Battles and Leaders of the Civil War*, 2:304.

89. Ibid.

90. *OR*, ser. 1, vol. 12, pt. 1, 381.

91. Ibid.

92. Allan, *History of the Campaign*, 49.

93. *OR*, ser. 1, vol. 12, pt. 1, 408.

94. Ecelbarger, *"We Are In for It!,"* 108–9.

95. *OR*, ser. 1, vol. 12, pt. 1, 394–95.

96. Ecelbarger, *"We Are In for It!,"* 108–9.

97. *OR*, ser. 1, vol. 12, pt. 1, 385.

98. McDonald, *Laurel Brigade*, 43.

99. *OR*, ser. 1, vol. 12, pt. 1, 360, 381; depending on the account, the time of the Confederate artillery bombardment varies. Colonel Kimball sets the time in his official report of the engagement at 4:00 p.m.

100. Ibid., 360.

101. Wood, *Seventh Regiment*, 98.

102. Mohr, ed., *Magnificent Irishman From Appalachia*, 16–17.

103. Rawling, *History of the First Regiment*, 62.

104. Wood, *Seventh Regiment*, 100–101.

105. Ecelbarger, *"We Are In for It!,"* 140.

106. Casler, *Four Years in the Stonewall Brigade*, 66.

107. *OR*, ser. 1, vol. 12, pt. 1, 409.

108. Sandie Pendleton to mother, March 29, 1862, quoted in Bean, ed., "Valley Campaign of 1862," 341–42.

109. Ibid.

110. *Farmer's Cabinet*, April 3, 1862.

111. Rawling, *History of the First Regiment*, 62.

112. Wood, *Seventh Regiment*, 102.

113. *OR*, ser. 1, vol. 12, pt. 1, 376.

114. Hinkley, *Narrative of Service*, 19.

115. Neese, *Three Years in the Confederate Horse Artillery*, 35.

116. *OR*, ser. 1, vol. 12, pt. 1, 376.

117. Fahrion, "Courage of a Virginia Color Bearer," 419.

118. Gainer Jr., *Ultimate Sacrifice at the Battle of Kernstown*, 58–60.

119. *OR*, ser. 1, vol. 12, pt. 1, 361.

120. Allan, *History of the Campaign*, 51.

121. Exchange quoted in Vandiver, *Mighty Stonewall*, 206–7.

122. Henderson, *Stonewall Jackson*, 186; Ecelbarger, *"We Are In for It!,"* 185–86.

123. Williamson, *Life of Thomas J. Jackson*, 132–33.

124. *OR*, ser. 1, vol. 12, pt. 1, 357.

125. Time-Life Books, eds., *Voices of the Civil War*, 52.

126. Casler, *Four Years in the Stonewall Brigade*, 67.

127. Neese, *Three Years in the Confederate Horse Artillery*, 36.

128. Stonewall Jackson to Mary Anna, March 24, 1862, quoted in Jackson, *Memoirs of Stonewall Jackson*, 243.

129. For a further, more detailed discussion of casualties at First Kernstown, see Ecelbarger, *"We Are In for It!,"* 273–77.

130. *OR*, ser. 1, vol. 12, pt. 1, 345.

131. John Peyton Clark Journal, March 24, 1862, Louisa Crawford Collection, HL.

132. Testimony of Randolph Martin, Pritchard Claim, Southern Claims Commission Reports, M1407, Nos. 4051–5053, National Archives and Records Administration, Washington, D.C.

133. Ibid.

134. Ibid., Southern Claims Commission Summary.

135. Gwin, ed., *A Woman's Civil War*, 37.

136. Laura Lee Diary, March 24, 1862, Swem Library, College of William and Mary, Williamsburg, Virginia.

137. Mary Greenhow Lee Diary, April 1, 1862, Mrs. Hugh Lee Collection, HL.

138. *Farmer's Cabinet*, April 3, 1862.

139. Ibid.; for a general discussion of burying the dead after battle, see Faust, *This Republic of Suffering*, 61–101.

140. *Philadelphia Press*, April 16, 1862; Sperry, *Surrender? Never Surrender!*, Kate Sperry Papers, HL.

141. Bean, ed., "Valley Campaign of 1862," 343.

142. John Peyton Clark Journal, March 24, 1862, Louisa Crawford Collection, HL.

143. Sperry, *Surrender? Never Surrender!*, Kate Sperry Papers, HL.

144. Seward observation quoted in Phipps, *Genteel Rebel*, 175.

145. Rawling, *History of the First Regiment*, 67.

146. *National Tribune*, August 22, 1907.

147. Ibid., March 26, 1885.

148. *OR*, ser. 1, vol. 12, pt. 1, 335–36.

149. SeCheverell, *Journal History of the Twenty-Ninth*, 40–41.

150. Wood, *Seventh Regiment*, 104–6.

151. *National Tribune*, August 22, 1907.

152. *The Blue and the Gray*, 21.

153. Robertson Jr., *Stonewall Jackson*, 347.

154. Avirett, *Memoirs of General Turner Ashby*, 164.

155. Robertson Jr., *Stonewall Jackson*, 349.

156. Bean, ed., "Valley Campaign of 1862," 344; for a detailed discussion of Garnett's removal from command, see "The Army of Northern Virginia's

Most Notorious Court-Martial," in Krick, *The Smoothbore Volley that Doomed the Confederacy*, 42–56.

157. Bean, ed., "Valley Campaign of 1862," 344.

158. Douglas, *I Rode with Stonewall*, 46.

159. Ibid.

160. Ibid.

# CHAPTER 3

161. Stephenson, "Jed Hotchkiss," 43–44; for the finest biographical treatment of Hotchkiss, see Miller, *Mapping for Stonewall*.

162. McDonald, ed., *Make Me a Map of the Valley*, 10.

163. Robertson Jr., *Stonewall Jackson*, 351; Davis, *Jefferson Davis*, 452–53; Cozzens, *Shenandoah 1862*, 234.

164. Casler, *Four Years in the Stonewall Brigade*, 69.

165. Ibid.

166. Ibid., 70; Robertson Jr., *Stonewall Jackson*, 351; Vandiver, *They Called Him Stonewall*, 215; Freeman, *Lee's Lieutenants*, 1:323; for an example of similar sentiment in Augusta County, see Ayers, *In the Presence of Mine Enemies*, 241–43.

167. Wenger and Rodes, comps., *Unionists and the Civil War Experience*, 2:15–16.

168. Jackson, *Memoirs of Stonewall Jackson*, 251.

169. Robertson Jr., *Stonewall Jackson*, 352.

170. Major R.W. Hunter quoted in Avirett, *Memoirs of General Turner Ashby*, 171.

171. McDonald, *History of the Laurel Brigade*, 49–50.

172. The strategic advantages of Conrad's Store and the selection process of this location are discussed at length in Robertson Jr., *Stonewall Jackson*, 356–57.

173. *OR*, ser. 1, vol. 12, pt. 1, 446.

174. Ibid.

175. Dwight, *Life and Letters of Wilder Dwight*, 235.

176. Ibid.

177. Noyalas, *"My Will Is Absolute Law,"* 37; Clemmer, *Old Alleghany*, 391–92, 394.

178. Dowdey and Manarin, eds., *Wartime Papers of R.E. Lee*, 151.

179. Wise, *Military History of the Virginia Military Institute*, 200.

180. *Macon Weekly Telegraph*, May 28, 1862.

181. Ibid.

182. Robertson, *Stonewall Brigade*, 84–85; Noyalas, *"My Will Is Absolute Law,"* 38.

183. *OR*, ser. 1, vol. 12, pt. 1, 465.

184. Ibid.

185. Ibid., 463.

186. Ibid.

187. Ibid.

188. Ibid.

189. Ibid., 465–66.

190. Ibid., 466.

191. Dabney, *Life and Campaigns*, 347.

192. *Daily Dispatch*, May 20, 1862.

193. General Robert H. Milroy to Mary Milroy, May 13, 1862, Robert H. Milroy Papers, Jasper County Public Library, Rensselaer, Indiana. Items from this collection hereafter cited as RHMJCPL.

194. *Daily Dispatch*, May 20, 1862.

195. *OR*, ser. 1, vol. 12, pt. 1, 466.

196. Hays, ed., *History of the Thirty-Second*, 24.

197. Alfred E. Lee, "Our First Battle: Bull Pasture Mountain," in Lamb, ed., *Magazine of American History*, 394–95.

198. Miller, "Grey Eagle on a Tether," 52.

199. Robertson Jr., *Stonewall Jackson*, 374–75.

200. Miller, "Grey Eagle on a Tether," 52.

201. *Macon Weekly Telegraph*, May 28, 1862.

202. *OR*, ser. 1, vol. 12, pt. 1, 483.

203. Howard, *Recollections of a Maryland Confederate Soldier*, 98.

204. *OR*, ser. 1, vol. 12, pt. 1, 469.

205. Milroy to Mary Milroy, May 13, 1862, RHMJCPL.

206. Cooke, *Life of Stonewall Jackson*, 84.

207. Milroy to Mary Milroy, May 13, 1862, RHMJCPL.

208. Dabney, *Life and Campaigns*, 348.

209. *OR*, ser. 1, vol. 12, pt. 1, 467.

210. Ibid., 464.

211. Robertson Jr., *Stonewall Jackson*, 376.

212. *OR*, ser. 1, vol. 12, pt. 1, 483.
213. Casler, *Four Years in the Stonewall Brigade*, 74.
214. Frank B. Jones Diary, May 13, 1862, Louisa Crawford Collection, HL.
215. McDonald, ed., *Make Me a Map of the Valley*, 43–44.
216. Avirett, *Memoirs of General Turner Ashby*, 181.
217. Worsham, *One of Jackson's Foot Cavalry*, 80.
218. *OR*, ser. 1, vol. 12, pt. 1, 473.
219. Dabney, *Life and Campaigns*, 350.
220. Jackson, *Memoirs of Stonewall Jackson*, 258.
221. Cooke, *Life of Stonewall Jackson*, 85.
222. Milroy to Mary Milroy, May 13, 1862, RHMJCPL.
223. Noyalas, *"My Will Is Absolute Law,"* 44.
224. Cooke, *Life of Stonewall Jackson*, 86.

# CHAPTER 4

225. General Robert E. Lee to General Thomas J. Stonewall Jackson, May 16, 1862, quoted in Dowdey and Manarin, eds., *Wartime Papers of R.E. Lee*, 174.
226. Ibid.
227. Buck, *With the Old Confeds*, 28.
228. Ewell's observations quoted in Freeman, *Lee's Lieutenants*, 1:350–51.
229. Allan, *History of the Campaign*, 88.
230. Cozzens, *Shenandoah 1862*, 281.
231. Buck, *With the Old Confeds*, 29.
232. Casler, *Four Years in the Stonewall Brigade*, 76.
233. Communication from Johnston to Ewell quoted in Freeman, *Lee's Lieutenants*, 1:371; in his biography of Jackson, Robertson presents a detailed examination of these communiqués and the issues they presented to Jackson. See Robertson Jr., *Stonewall Jackson*, 388–89.
234. Taylor, *Destruction and Reconstruction*, 52–53.
235. Beck and Grunder, *First Battle of Winchester*, 26.
236. The numerical figures for the size of Banks's command are derived from a communication that Banks sent to the War Department on May 21, 1862. Banks stated that he had 4,476 infantry at Strasburg, along with 1,600 cavalry. Additionally, Banks had about 1,000 men at Front Royal. See *OR*, ser. 1, vol. 12, pt. 1, 523.

237. Bushong, *General Turner Ashby*, 122.

238. *OR*, ser. 1, vol. 12, pt. 1, 524.

239. Ibid., 536.

240. Ibid., 522.

241. Ibid., 524.

242. Ibid.

243. Ecelbarger, *Three Days in the Shenandoah*, 24–25.

244. *OR*, ser. 1, vol. 12, pt. 1, 524.

245. Eby Jr., ed., *A Virginia Yankee in the Civil War*, 35.

246. Hinkley, *Narrative of Service*, 21–22.

247. Bushong, *General Turner Ashby*, 120–21.

248. Battle of Front Royal Committee, *"Brother Against Brother,"* 20–23; Robertson Jr., *Stonewall Jackson*, 395.

249. McKim, *A Soldier's Recollections*, 97.

250. Robertson Jr., *Stonewall Jackson*, 395.

251. McKim, *A Soldier's Recollections*, 96.

252. *Public Ledger*, May 27, 1862.

253. Ibid.

254. Boyd, *Belle Boyd in Camp and Prison*, 119, 123; Douglas, *I Rode with Stonewall*, 59.

255. *Sun*, May 31, 1862.

256. Camper and Kirkley, comps., *Historical Record of the First Regiment*, 32.

257. Ibid., 33; *OR*, ser. 1, vol. 12, pt. 1, 555–56.

258. Toomey, *Hero at Front Royal*, 48.

259. McKim, *A Soldier's Recollections*, 97.

260. Ashby, *Valley Campaign*, 118–19.

261. McKim, *A Soldier's Recollections*, 96.

262. Buck, *Sad Earth, Sweet Heaven*, 81.

263. Beyer and Keydel, *Deeds of Valor*, 30–31.

264. Beck and Grunder, *First Battle of Winchester*, 31; Roberston, *Stonewall Jackson*, 397.

265. Toomey, *Hero at Front Royal*, 52.

266. Camper and Kirkley, comps., *Historical Record of the First Regiment*, 39.

267. Toomey, *Hero at Front Royal*, 52–53; the Confederates captured 903 Federals of 1,063 engaged at Front Royal.

268. *Southern Historical Society Papers* 8 (1880): 333–34.

269. Toomey, *Hero at Front Royal*, 55.

270. *Philadelphia Inquirer*, June 6, 1862.

271. Toomey, *Hero at Front Royal*, 57.

272. William J. Miller, "Such Men as Shields, Banks, and Fremont: Federal Command in Western Virginia, March–June 1862," in Gallagher, ed., *Shenandoah Valley Campaign of 1862*, 56–57.

273. Gordon, *Brook Farm to Cedar Mountain*, 193.

274. Eby Jr., ed., *A Virginia Yankee in the Civil War*, 38.

275. Gordon, *Brook Farm to Cedar Mountain*, 193.

276. *OR*, ser. 1, vol. 12, pt. 1, 526.

277. Hagerty, *Collis' Zouaves*, 46.

278. *OR*, ser. 1, vol. 12, pt. 1, 527.

279. Noyalas, *Plagued by War*, 50–51.

280. Allan, *History of the Campaign*, 102.

281. Marvin, *Fifth Regiment Connecticut Volunteers*, 97.

282. *OR*, ser. 1, vol. 12, pt. 1, 568.

283. Charles W. Boyce Journal, 74, Boyce Papers, Library of Congress, Washington, D.C.

284. *OR*, ser. 1, vol. 12, pt. 1, 605.

285. Barton, "The Battle at Winchester," Virginia Historical Society, Richmond, Virginia.

286. Tobie, *History of the First Maine Cavalry*, 36.

287. McDonald, *History of the Laurel Brigade*, 61.

288. *OR*, ser. 1, vol. 12, pt. 1, 703.

289. Testimony of Caroline Heater, Heater Claim Brief on Loyalty, Belle Grove Collection, Box 13, HL.

290. Hagerty, *Collis' Zouaves*, 47; Cozzens, *Shenandoah 1862*, 327.

291. *Philadelphia Inquirer*, May 31, 1862.

292. Ibid.; Hagerty, *Collis' Zouaves*, 47–51.

293. Laura Lee Diary, May 24, 1862, Swem Library, College of William and Mary, Williamsburg, Virginia.

294. Julia Chase Diary, May 24, 1862, Julia Chase Collection, HL.

295. Laura Lee Diary, May 24, 1862, Swem Library, College of William and Mary, Williamsburg, Virginia.

296. Quaife, ed., *From the Cannon's Mouth*, 79.

297. Julia Chase Diary, May 24, 1862, Julia Chase Collection, HL.

298. Collier, ed., *Letters of a Civil War Soldier*, 158.

299. *National Tribune*, August 20, 1896.

300. *OR*, ser. 1, vol. 12, pt. 1, 794.

301. Beck and Grunder, *First Battle of Winchester*, 51.

302. *Philadelphia Press*, June 4, 1862.

303. Beck and Grunder, *First Battle of Winchester*, 51.

304. Marvin, *Fifth Regiment Connecticut Volunteers*, 101.

305. Ibid., 102.

306. Collier, ed., *Letters of a Civil War Soldier*, 158.

307. *Philadelphia Inquirer*, May 30, 1862.

308. Robertson Jr., *Stonewall Jackson*, 405.

309. Barton, "War Memoirs," 79, Robert Barton Family Papers, HL.

310. Taylor, *Destruction and Reconstruction*.

311. Ibid.

312. Ibid., 67.

313. Ibid.

314. Ibid.

315. Gordon, *Brook Farm to Cedar Mountain*, 237–38.

316. *OR*, ser. 1, vol. 12, pt. 1, 617.

317. Worsham, *One of Jackson's Foot Cavalry*, 87.

318. Ibid.

319. Douglas, *I Rode with Stonewall*, 66.

320. McKim, *A Soldier's Recollections*, 101.

321. *OR*, ser. 1, vol. 12, pt. 1, 617.

322. Ibid., 580.

323. *National Tribune*, November 17, 1887; George Nye to Mother, May 29, 1862, George Nye Papers, Nicholas P. Picerno private collection, Bridgewater, Virginia. In the letter to his mother, Nye stated that Confederate artillery, during the Union retreat, "were throwing in their shell and shot like rain."

324. *Philadelphia Inquirer*, May 30, 1862.

325. Collier, ed., *Letters of a Civil War Soldier*, 159.

326. Duncan, ed., *Blue-Eyed Child of Fortune*, 204.

327. *Philadelphia Inquirer*, May 30, 1862.

328. Collier, ed., *Letters of a Civil War Soldier*, 166.

329. Jackson, *Memoirs of Stonewall Jackson*, 263.

330. Barton, "War Memoirs," 81, Robert Barton Family Papers, HL.

331. Letter of Commissary Sergeant, 5th Connecticut Volunteer Infantry, May 28, 1862, Rufus Mead Papers, Container 1, Library of Congress, Washington, D.C.

332. *Philadelphia Inquirer*, May 31, 1862.

333. Neese, *Three Years in the Confederate Horse Artillery*, 61.

334. Allan, *History of the Campaign*, 115.

335. Buck, *With the Old Confeds*, 31.

336. Ibid.

337. Noyalas, *Plagued by War*, 58.

338. Allan, *History of the Campaign*, 115.

339. Ibid., 116, 118; Robertson Jr., *Stonewall Jackson*, 411.

340. Duncan, ed, *Blue-Eyed Child of Fortune*, 204.

341. Quint, *Potomac and Rapidan*, 151.

342. Quaife, ed., *From the Cannon's Mouth*, 88–90.

343. Basler, ed., *Collected Works of Abraham Lincoln*, 5:235–36.

344. Huntington, "Winchester to Port Republic," 1:321.

345. Ibid., 318.

346. *Richmond Examiner*, May 27, 1862.

347. Mary Greenhow Lee Diary, May 27, 1862, Mrs. Hugh Lee Collection, HL.

# CHAPTER 5

348. *OR*, ser. 1, vol. 12, pt. 1, 643.

349. Miller, "Such Men as Shields, Banks, and Fremont," in Gallagher, ed., *Shenandoah Valley Campaign of 1862*, 67.

350. *OR*, ser. 1, vol. 12, pt. 1, 644.

351. Ibid.

352. Ibid., 647.

353. Buck, *Sad Earth, Sweet Heaven*, 88–89.

354. *OR*, ser. 1, vol. 12, pt. 1, 694.

355. Laura Lee Diary, May 30, 1862, Swem Library, College of William and Mary, Williamsburg, Virginia.

356. Sperry, *Surrender? Never Surrender!*, May 31, 1862, Kate Sperry Papers, HL.

357. *OR*, ser. 1, vol. 12, pt. 1, 708.

358. Cozzens, *Shenandoah 1862*, 414–15.

359. Noyalas, *"My Will Is Absolute Law,"* 46.

360. Tanner, *Stonewall in the Valley*, 278–79; Robertson Jr., *Stonewall Jackson*, 426.

361. Heneberger, ed., *Harrisonburg, Virginia*, June 6, 1862.

362. *New York Times*, June 22, 1862.

363. Ibid.

364. Avirett, *Memoirs of General Turner Ashby*, 219–20.

365. McDonald, *History of the Laurel Brigade*, 67.

366. Avirett, *Memoirs of General Turner Ashby*, 222–23.

367. Ibid., 223.

368. Jackson, *Memoirs of Stonewall Jackson*, 271.

369. Avirett, *Memoirs of General Turner Ashby*, 227.

370. *Baltimore Sun*, June 7, 1898.

371. Milroy to Mary Milroy, June 15, 1862, RHMJCPL.

372. Dabney, *Life and Campaigns*, 411.

373. Robertson Jr., *Stonewall Jackson*, 433–34.

374. Oates, *War Between the United States and the Confederacy*, 103.

375. *OR*, ser. 1, vol. 12, pt. 1, 795.

376. Ibid., 19.

377. Ibid., 781.

378. Ibid., 795.

379. Ibid.

380. Ibid., 728.

381. *New York Times*, June 20, 1862.

382. Ibid., June 17, 1862.

383. Wayland, ed., "Fremont's Pursuit of Jackson," 334.

384. Milroy to Mary Milroy, June 15, 1862, RHMJCPL; Krick, *Conquering the Valley*, 146, 149–50.

385. Milroy to Mary Milroy, June 15, 1862, RHMJCPL.

386. *OR*, ser. 1, vol. 12, pt. 1, 20.

387. Ibid., 796.

388. Ibid.

389. *Richmond Daily Dispatch*, June 21, 1862.

390. Milroy to Mary Milroy, June 15, 1862, RHMJCPL.

391. *Confederate Veteran* (July 1895), 213.

392. Buck, *With the Old Confeds*, 36.

393. Milroy to Mary Milroy, June 15, 1862, RHMJCPL.

394. Noyalas, *"My Will Is Absolute Law,"* 51.

395. Milroy to Mary Milroy, June 15, 1862, RHMJCPL.

396. *New York Times*, June 16, 1862.

397. Bayard, *Life of General Dashiell Bayard*, 218.

398. *OR*, ser. 1, vol. 12, pt. 1, 21.

399. Allan, *History of the Campaign*, 156.

400. *New York Times*, June 16, 1862.

401. Ibid.

402. *OR*, ser. 1, vol. 12, pt. 1, 797.

403. Ibid.

404. *Richmond Daily Dispatch*, June 21, 1862.

405. *OR*, ser. 1, vol. 12, pt. 1, 798.

406. Ibid., 714; Dabney, *Life and Campaigns*, 422.

407. *OR*, ser. 1, vol. 12, pt. 1, 714.

408. Krick, *Conquering the Valley*, 322.

409. *OR*, ser. 1, vol. 12, pt. 1, 714.

410. Tanner, *Stonewall in the Valley*, 298.

411. SeCheverell, *Journal History of the Twenty-Ninth*, 47.

412. Ibid., 46.

413. Wood, *Seventh Regiment*, 117.

414. SeCheverell, *Journal History of the Twenty-Ninth*, 46.

415. Dabney, *Life and Campaigns*, 423.

416. Barton, "War Memoirs," 95, Robert Barton Family Papers, HL.

417. *OR*, ser. 1, vol. 12, pt. 1, 714–15.

418. Allan, *History of the Campaign*, 159.

419. McDonald, ed., *Make Me a Map of the Valley*, 55; Roberston, *Stonewall Jackson*, 443; Collins, *Battles of Cross Keys and Port Republic*, 103–4; Taylor, *Destruction and Reconstruction*, 90–91.

420. *Confederate Veteran* (September 1904), 430.

421. Rawling, *History of the First Regiment*, 96.

422. Huntington, "Winchester to Port Republic," 1:322.

423. Neese, *Three Years in the Confederate Horse Artillery*, 74.

424. Buck, *With the Old Confeds*, 38.

425. Taylor, *Destruction and Reconstruction*, 92.

426. Tanner, *Stonewall in the Valley*, 304–5; there seems to be some slight discrepancy over the number of assaults it took for Taylor to successfully secure the position. Taylor, as well as modern historians, states that it was three. Collins suggests that it was four assaults.

427. Neese, *Three Years in the Confederate Horse Artillery*, 74.

428. Collins, *Battles of Cross Keys and Port Republic*, 111.

429. Buck, *With the Old Confeds*, 38.

430. Oates, *War Between the United States and the Confederacy*, 105.

431. Neese, *Three Years in the Confederate Horse Artillery*, 76.

432. Clara Strayer Diary, quoted in Time-Life, eds., *Voices of the Civil War*, 142–43.

433. Huntington, "Winchester to Port Republic," 337.

434. Mohr, ed., *Magnificent Irishman from Appalachia*, 36.

435. Huntington, "Winchester to Port Republic," 337.

436. Jackson, *Memoirs of Stonewall Jackson*, 282.

437. Dabney to wife, June 12, 1862, quoted in Johnson, *Life and Letters of Robert Lewis Dabney*, 266.

438. "An English Combatant," *Battle-Fields of the South*, 294–95.

# Chapter 6

439. For a discussion of the importance of the timing of Jackson's victories in the valley to cement his legacy, see Gallagher, *Lee and His Generals*, 101–117.

440. Woodward, ed., *Mary Chestnut's Civil War*, 361.

441. Ibid.

442. Reverend C.C. Jones to Lieutenant Charles C. Jones Jr., May 28, 1862, quoted in Myers, *Children of Pride*, 248.

443. Judith Brockenbrough McGuire Diary, quoted in Davis and Robertson Jr., eds., *Virginia at War*, 183.

444. Myers, *Children of Pride*, 258.

445. Graham, "Some Reminiscences of Stonewall Jackson," 77.

446. Cooke, *Stonewall Jackson*, 195.

447. Stephens, *Constitutional View of the Late War*, 2:452.

448. *New York Times*, June 16, 1862.

449. Robert K. Krick, "The Metamorphosis in Stonewall Jackson's Public Image," in Gallagher, ed., *Shenandoah Valley Campaign of 1862*, 24.

450. For further discussion of Jackson during the Seven Days, see Robert K. Krick, "Sleepless in the Saddle: Stonewall Jackson in the Seven Days," in Gallagher, ed., *Richmond Campaign of 1862*, 66–95.

451. Myers, *Children of Pride*, 373.

452. Mary Greenhow Lee Diary, May 13, 1863, Mrs. Hugh Lee Collection, HL.

453. Sperry, *Surrender? Never Surrender!*, May 13, 1863, Kate Sperry Papers, HL.

454. Garner, *Civil War World of Herman Melville*, 242–43.

455. Nicolay and Hay, *Complete Works of Abraham Lincoln*, 5:393.

456. Basler, ed., *Collected Works of Abraham Lincoln*, 6:214.

457. Davis, *Cause Lost*, 162; Hopley, *"Stonewall" Jackson*, 42–97.

458. Luvaas, ed., *Civil War: A Soldier's View*, 295.

459. Gallagher, ed., *Fighting for the Confederacy*, 94.

460. Holzer and Neely Jr., *Mine Eyes Have Seen the Glory*, 66–67; Simms Jr., "Nineteenth Century Virginia Portraiture," 25.

461. Stevenson, *Confederate Soldier Artists*, 63, 73; Neely Jr., Holzer and Boritt, *Confederate Image*, 206; Holzer and Neely Jr., *Mine Eyes Have Seen the Glory*, 148.

462. Clark, *Civilisation*, 1.

463. Townsend, *Rustics in Rebellion*, 215–16.

464. For examples of modern-day admiration for Stonewall Jackson, see Gallagher, *Causes Won, Lost, & Forgotten*, 136–38, 143–44, 156–58.

465. Jackson, *Memoirs of Stonewall Jackson*, 284.

# Bibliography

## Manuscript Collections

Jasper County Public Library, Rensselaer, Indiana.
   Robert H. Milroy Papers.

Jonathan A. Noyalas, Martinsburg, West Virginia.
   Baltimore & Ohio Railroad Brochure

Library of Congress, Washington, D.C.
   Boyce Papers
   Rufus Mead Papers

National Archives and Records Administration, Washington, D.C.
   Southern Claims Commission Reports, M1407

Nicholas P. Picerno, Bridgewater, Virginia.
   George Nye Papers

Stewart Bell Jr. Archives, Handley Library, Winchester, Virginia.
   Belle Grove Collection
   Julia Chase Collection
   Kate Sperry Papers
   Louisa Crawford Collection

Mrs. Hugh Lee Collection
Robert Barton Family Papers

Swem Library, College of William and Mary, Williamsburg, Virginia.
Laura Lee Diary

Virginia Historical Society, Richmond, Virginia.
Robert T. Barton, "The Battle at Winchester"

## GOVERNMENT DOCUMENTS

U.S. War Department, comp. *War of the Rebellion: A Compilation of the Official Records of the Union and Confederate Armies*. 128 vols. Washington, D.C.: U.S. Government Printing Office, 1880–1901.

## PUBLISHED PRIMARY SOURCES

Allan, William. *History of the Campaign of Gen. T.J. (Stonewall) Jackson in the Shenandoah Valley of Virginia*. London: Hughes Reed Ltd., 1912.

"An English Combatant." *Battle-Fields of the South, From Bull Run to Fredericksburgh: With Sketches of Confederate Commanders, and Gossip of the Camps*. New York: John Bradburn, 1864.

Ashby, Thomas A. *The Valley Campaigns: Being the Reminiscences of a Non-Combatant While Between the Lines in the Shenandoah Valley During the War of the States*. New York: Neale Publishing Co., 1914.

Avirett, James B. *The Memoirs of General Turner Ashby and His Compeers*. Baltimore, MD: Selby and Dulany, 1867.

Basler, Roy P. *The Collected Works of Abraham Lincoln*. Vols. 5 and 6. New Brunswick, NJ: Rutgers University Press, 1953.

Bayard, Samuel J. *The Life of General Dashiell Bayard: Late Captain, U.S.A., and Brigadier General of Volunteers, Killed in the Battle of Fredericksburg, Dec. 1862*. New York: G.P. Putnam's Sons, 1874.

Bean, William G., ed. "The Valley Campaign of 1862 as Revealed in the Letters of Sandie Pendleton." *Virginia Magazine of History and Biography* 78, no. 3 (1970): 326–364.

Boyd, Belle. *Belle Boyd in Camp and Prison*. New York: Blelock & Co., 1866.

Buck, Lucy. *Sad Earth, Sweet Heaven: The Diary of Lucy Rebecca Buck During the War Between the States, Front Royal, Virginia, December 25, 1861–April 15, 1865.* Birmingham, AL: Buck Publishing Co., 1992.

Buck, Samuel D. *With the Old Confeds: Actual Experiences of a Captain in the Line.* Baltimore, MD: H.E. Houck, 1925.

Camper, Charles, and J.W. Kirkley, comps. *Historical Record of the First Regiment Maryland Infantry, with an Appendix Containing a Register of the Officers and Enlisted Men, Biographies of Deceased Officers, etc.* Washington, D.C.: Gibson Brothers, Printers, 1871.

Casler, John O. *Four Years in the Stonewall Brigade.* Girard, KS: Appeal Publishing Co., 1906.

Cockrell, Monroe F. *Gunner with Stonewall: Reminiscences of William Thomas Poague.* Wilmington, NC: Broadfoot, 1989.

Collier, Ellen C., ed. *Letters of a Civil War Soldier: Chandler B. Gilliam, 28th New York Volunteers, with Diary of W.L. Hicks.* Bloomington, IN: Xlibris, 2005.

Cooke, John Esten. *The Life of Stonewall Jackson: From Official Papers, Contemporary Narratives.* New York: Rennie, Shea and Lindsey, 1868.

————. *Stonewall Jackson: A Military Biography, with a Portrait and Maps.* New York: D. Appleton and Co., 1866.

Dabney, Professor R.L., DD. *Life and Campaigns of Lieut-Gen. Thomas J. Jackson.* New York: Blelock and Co., 1866.

Douglas, Henry Kyd. *I Rode with Stonewall.* Marietta, GA: Mockingbird Books, 1995.

Dowdey, Clifford, and Louis H. Manarin, eds. *The Wartime Papers of R.E. Lee.* New York: Bramhall House, 1961.

Duncan, Russell, ed. *Blue-Eyed Child of Fortune: The Civil War Letters of Colonel Robert Gould Shaw.* Athens: University of Georgia Press, 1992.

Dwight, Theodore F. *Campaigns in Virginia, 1861–1862: Papers of the Military Historical Society of Masachusetts.* Boston, MA: James R. Osgood and Co., 1881.

Dwight, Wilder. *Life and Letters of Wilder Dwight.* Boston, MA: Ticknor and Fields, 1868.

Eby, Cecil D., Jr., ed. *A Virginia Yankee in the Civil War: The Diaries of David Hunter Strother.* Chapel Hill: University of North Carolina Press, 1961.

Fahrion, C.W., Lieutenant. "Courage of a Virginia Color Bearer." *Confederate Veteran* 17, no. 3 (1909): 419.

Farrar, Samuel Clark. *The Twenty-Second Pennsylvania Cavalry and the Ringgold Battalion, 1861–1865*. N.p.: Published under the Auspices of the Twenty-Second Pennsylvania Ringgold Cavalry Association, 1911.

Gallagher, Gary W., ed. *Fighting for the Confederacy: The Personal Recollections of General Edward Porter Alexander*. Chapel Hill: University of North Carolina Press, 1989.

Gates, Betsey, ed. *The Colton Letters: Civil War Period, 1861–1865*. Scottsdale, AZ: McClane Publications, 1993.

Gordon, George H. *Brook Farm to Cedar Mountain: In the War of the Great Rebellion, 1861–1862*. Boston, MA: Houghton, Mifflin and Co., 1885.

Graham, James R., Reverend. "Some Reminiscences of Stonewall Jackson." *Winchester-Frederick County Historical Society Journal* 11 (1998–99): 77–102.

Gwin, Minrose C., ed. *A Woman's Civil War: A Diary with Reminiscences of War, From March 1862*. Madison: University of Wisconsin Press, 1992.

Hays, E.Z., ed. *History of the Thirty-Second Regiment Ohio Veteran Volunteer Infantry*. Columbus, OH: Cott & Evans, Printers, 1896.

Heneburger, E.R. Grymes, ed. *Harrisonburg, Virginia: Diary of a Citizens from May 9, 1862–August 22, 1864*. Harrisonburg, VA, 1961.

Hinkley, Julian Wisner. *A Narrative of Service with the Third Wisconsin Infantry*. N.p.: Wisconsin History Commission, 1912.

Howard, McHenry. *Recollections of a Maryland Confederate Soldier and Staff Officer under Johnston, Jackson, and Lee*. Baltimore, MD: Williams and Wilkins, Co., 1914.

Huntington, James F. "Operations in the Shenandoah Valley, From Winchester to Port Republic, 1862." *Papers of the Military Historical Society of Massachusetts*. Boston, MA: James R. Osgood and Co., 1881.

Jackson, Mary Anna. *Memoirs of Stonewall Jackson*. Louisville, KY: Courier-Journal Printing Co., 1895.

Johnson, Clifton. *Battleground Adventures: The Stories of Dwellers on the Scenes of Conflict in Some of the Most Notable Battles of the Civil War*. Boston, MA: Houghton Mifflin, 1915.

Johnson, Robert Underwood, and Clarence Clough Buel, eds. *Battles and Leaders of the Civil War*. Vol. 2. New York: Century, 1888.

Johnson, Thomas Clary. *The Life and Letters of Robert Lewis Dabney*. Richmond, VA: Presbyterians Committee on Publication, 1903.

Johnston, Joseph E. *Narrative of Military Operations Directed during the Late War Between the States*. New York: D. Appleton and Co., 1874.

Jones, J. William, Reverend, DD, comp. *Army of Northern Virginia Memorial Volume*. Richmond, VA: J.W. Randolph & English, 1880.

Lamb, Martha J., ed. *Magazine of American History with Notes and Queries*. New York: Historical Pub. Co., 1886.

Marvin, Edward E. *The Fifth Connecticut Volunteers: A History Compiled from Diaries and Official Reports*. Hartford, CT: Press of Wiley, Waterman, and Eaton, 1889.

McDonald, Archie P., ed. *Make Me a Map of the Valley: The Civil War Journals of Stonewall Jackson's Topographer*. Dallas, TX: Southern Methodist University Press, 1973.

McDonald, William N., Captain. *A History of the Laurel Brigade: Originally the Ashby Cavalry of the Army of Northern Virginia*. N.p.: Mrs. Kate S. McDonald, 1907.

McKim, Randolph H. *A Soldier's Recollections: Leaves from the Diary of a Young Confederate*. New York: Longmans, Green and Co., 1910.

Mohr, Julian, ed. *A Magnificent Irishman from Appalachia: The Letters of James Gildea, First Ohio Light Artillery, Battery L*. Milford: OH: Little Miami Publishing Co., 2003.

Myers, Robert Manson. *The Children of Pride: A True Story of Georgia and the Civil War*. New Haven, CT: Yale University Press, 1972.

Neese, George M. *Three Years in the Confederate Horse Artillery*. New York: Neale Publishing Co., 1911.

Nicolay, John G., and John Hay, eds. *Complete Works of Abraham Lincoln*. Vol. 7. New York: Tandy-Thomas Co., 1905.

Oates, William C. *The War Between the United States and the Confederacy and Its Lost Opportunities, With a History of the 15th Alabama Regiment*. New York: Neale Publishing Co., 1905.

Opie, John N. *A Rebel Cavalryman with Lee Stuart and Jackson*. Chicago, IL: W.B. Conkey, 1899.

Quaife, Milo M., ed. *From the Cannon's Mouth: The Civil War Letters of General Alpheus Williams*. Detroit, MI: Wayne State University Press and the Detroit Historical Society, 1959.

Quint, Alonzo H. *The Potomac and Rapidan: Army Notes, from the Failure at Winchester to the Reenforcement of Rosecrans, 1861–3*. Boston: Crosby and Nichols, 1864.

Rawling, C.J. *History of the First Regiment Virginia Infantry*. Philadelphia, PA: J.B. Lippincott, 1887.

Sears, Stephen W., ed. *The Civil War Papers of George B. McClellan: Selected Correspondence 1861–1865*. New York: DaCapo Press, 1992.

SeCheverell, J. Hamp. *Journal History of the Twenty-Ninth Ohio Veteran Volunteers, 1861–1865, Its Victories and Its Reverses*. Cleveland, OH: self-published, 1883.

*Southern Historical Society Papers*. 52 vols. Richmond, VA: Southern Historical Society, 1876–1952.

Stephens, Alexander H. *A Constitutional View of the Late War Between the States: Its Causes, Character, Conduct, and Results, Presented in a Series of Colloquies at Liberty Hall*. 2 vols. Philadelphia, PA: National Publishing Co., 1870.

Taylor, Richard. *Destruction and Reconstruction: Personal Reminiscences of the Late War in the United States*. Edinburg: William Blackford and Sons, 1879.

Time-Life Books, eds. *Voices of the Civil War: Shenandoah 1862*. Alexandria, VA: Time-Life Books, 1997.

Tobie, Edward P. *History of the First Maine Cavalry: 1861–1865*. Boston, MA: Press of Emery and Hughes, 1887.

Townsend, George Alfred. *Rustics in Rebellion: A Yankee Reporter on the Road to Richmond, 1861–65*. Chapel Hill: University of North Carolina Press, 1950.

Trowbridge, J.T. *The South: A Tour of Its Battle-Fields and Ruined Cities, A Journey Through the Desolated States, and Talks with the People*. Hartford, CT: L. Stebbins, 1866.

Wayland, Francis F., ed. "Fremont's Pursuit of Jackson in the Shenandoah Valley: The Journal of Colonel Albert Tracy, March–July 1862." *Virginia Magazine of History and Biography* 70 (1962): 332–54.

Wenger, Norman R., and David S. Rodes, comps. *Unionists and the Civil War Experience in the Shenandoah Valley: Greenmont, Edom, and Linville, Rockingham County, Virginia*. Harrisonburg, VA: Valley Brethren-Mennonite Heritage Center and the Valley Research Associates, 2004.

Wood, George L., Major. *The Seventh Regiment: A Record*. New York: James Miller, 1865.

Woodward, C. Vann, ed. *Mary Chestnut's Civil War*. New York: Esssential Classics of the Civil War, 1994.

Worsham, John H. *One of Jackson's Foot Cavalry: His Experiences and What He Saw During the War, 1861–1865*. New York: Neale Publishing Co., 1912.

# NEWSPAPERS

*Baltimore Sun*
*Daily Dispatch*
*Farmer's Cabinet*
*Macon Weekly Telegraph*
*National Tribune*
*New York Times*
*Patriot*
*Philadelphia Inquirer*
*Philadelphia Press*
*Public Ledger*
*Richmond Daily Dispatch*
*Richmond Examiner*
*The Sun*

# SECONDARY SOURCES

Anderson, Paul Christopher. *Blood Image: Turner Ashby in the Civil War and the Southern Mind*. Baton Rouge: Louisiana State University Press, 2002.

Ayers, Edward L. *In the Presence of Mine Enemies: War in the Heart of America, 1859–1863*. New York: W.W. Norton & Co., 2003.

Battle of Front Royal Committee. *"Brother Against Brother": The Battle of Front Royal, May 23, 1862*. Front Royal, VA: Battle of Front Royal Committee, 2003.

Beck, Brandon H., and Charles S. Grunder. *The First Battle of Winchester*. Lynchburg, VA: H.E. Howard, 1992.

Berkey, Jonathan M. "War in the Borderland: The Civilians' Civil War in Virginia's Lower Shenandoah Valley." PhD dissertation, Pennsylvania State University, 2003.

Beyer, W.F., and O.F. Keydel. *Deeds of Valor: How America's Civil War Heroes Won the Congressional Medal of Honor*. New York: Smithmark, 2000.

Bushong, Millard K. *General Turner Ashby and Stonewall's Valley Campaign*. Berryville, VA: Virginia Book Co., 1980.

Clark, Kenneth. *Civilisation*. New York: Harper & Row, 1969.

Clemmer, Gregg S. *Old Alleghany: The Life and Wars of General Ed Johnson*. Staunton, VA: Hearthside, 2004.

Collins, Darrell L. *The Battles of Cross Keys and Port Republic*. Lynchburg, VA: H.E. Howard, 1993.

Cozzens, Peter. *Shenandoah 1862: Stonewall Jackson's 1862 Valley Campaign*. Chapel Hill: University of North Carolina Press, 2008.

Davis, William C. *The Cause Lost: Myths and Realities of the Confederacy*. Lawrence: University Press of Kansas, 1996.

———. *Jefferson Davis: The Man and His Hour*. New York: Harper Collins, 1991.

Davis, William C., and James I. Robertson Jr., eds. *Virginia at War: 1862*. Lexington: University Press of Kentucky, 2007.

Ecelbarger, Gary L. *Three Days in the Shenandoah: Stonewall Jackson at Front Royal and Winchester*. Norman: University of Oklahoma Press, 2008.

———. *"We Are In for It!": The First Battle of Kernstown*. Shippensburg, PA: White Mane Publishing, 1997.

Faust, Drew Gilpin. *This Republic of Suffering: Death and the American Civil War*. New York: Alfred A. Knopf, 2008.

Freeman, Douglas Southall. *Lee's Lieutenants*. Vol. 1. New York: Charles Scribner's Sons, 1943.

Gainer, Roderick Rodgers, Jr. *Ultimate Sacrifice at the Battle of Kernstown: William Gray Murray, First Pennsylvania Colonel to Die in the American Civil War*. Shippensburg, PA: White Mane Publishing, 2007.

Gallagher, Gary W. *Causes Won, Lost, & Forgotten: How Hollywood and Popular Art Shape What We Know About the Civil War*. Chapel Hill: University of North Carolina Press, 2008.

———. *Lee and His Generals in War and Memory*. Baton Rouge: Louisiana State University Press, 1998.

Gallagher, Gary W., ed. *The Richmond Campaign of 1862: The Peninsula & Seven Days*. Chapel Hill: University of North Carolina Press, 2000.

———. *The Shenandoah Valley Campaign of 1862*. Chapel Hill: University of North Carolina Press, 2003.

Garner, Stanton. *The Civil War World of Herman Melville*. Lawrence: University Press of Kansas, 1993.

Greene, A. Wilson. *Whatever You Resolve to Be: Essays on Stonewall Jackson*. Baltimore, MD: Butternut and Blue, 1992.

Hagerty, Edward J. *Collis' Zouaves: The 114th Pennsylvania Volunteers in the Civil War*. Baton Rouge: Louisiana State University Press, 1997.

Henderson, G.F.R. *Stonewall Jackson and the American Civil War*. New York: DaCapo, 1989.

Holzer, Harold, and Mark E. Neely Jr. *Mine Eyes Have Seen the Glory: The Civil War in Art*. New York: Orion Books, 1993.

Hopley, Catherine Cooper. *"Stonewall" Jackson, General of the Confederate States Arrmy: A Biographical Sketch, and an Outline of His Virginian Campaigns*. London: Chapman and Hall, 1863.

Inscoe, John C., and Robert C. Kenzer, eds. *Enemies of the Country: New Perspectives on Unionists in the Civil War South*. Athens: University of Georgia Press, 2001.

Krick, Robert K. *Conquering the Valley: Stonewall Jackson at Port Republic*. Baton Rouge: Louisiana State University Press, 1996.

————. *The Smoothbore Volley that Doomed the Confederacy: The Death of Stonewall Jackson and Other Chapters on the Army of Northern Virginia*. Baton Rouge: Louisiana State University Press, 2002.

Luvaas, Jay, ed. *The Civil War: A Soldier's View, A Collection of Civil War Writings by Col. G.F.R. Henderson*. Chicago, IL: University of Chicago Press, 1958.

May, George Elliott. *Port Republic: The History of a Shenandoah Valley River Town*. Port Republic, VA: Society of Port Republic Preservationists, 2002.

Miller, William J. "Grey Eagle on a Tether." *America's Civil War* 15, no. 5 (2002): 46–52, 88.

————. *Mapping for Stonewall: The Civil War Service of Jed Hotchkiss*. Washington, D.C.: Elliott & Clark Publishing, 1993.

Neely, Mark E., Jr., Harold Holzer and Gabor S. Boritt. *The Confederate Image: Portraits of the Lost Cause*. Chapel Hill: University of North Carolina Press, 1987.

Noyalas, Jonathan A., ed. *Home Front to Front Line: The Civil War Era in the Shenandoah Valley*. New Market, VA: Shenandoah Valley Battlefields Foundation, 2009.

————. *"My Will Is Absolute Law": A Biography of Union General Robert H. Milroy*. Jefferson, NC: McFarland, 2006.

————. *Plagued by War: Winchester, Virginia, During the Civil War*. Leesburg, VA: Gauley Mount Press, 2003.

————. "Portrait of a Soldier: The Confederate Military Service of Private Robert T. Barton, 1861–1862." *Winchester-Frederick County Historical Society Journal* 16 (2004): 73–94.

————. *Two Peoples, One Community: The African American Experience in Newtown (Stephens City), Virginia, 1850–1870*. Stephens City, VA: Stone House Foundation, 2007.

Parrish, T. Michael. *Richard Taylor: Soldier Prince of Dixie*. Chapel Hill: University of North Carolina Press, 1992.

Phipps, Sheila R. *Genteel Rebel: The Life of Mary Greenhow Lee*. Baton Rouge: Louisiana State University Press, 2004.

Robertson, James I., Jr. *The Stonewall Brigade*. Baton Rouge: Louisiana State University Press, 1963.

———. *Stonewall Jackson: The Man, The Soldier, The Legend*. New York: Macmillan, 1997.

Rowland, Thomas J. *George B. McClellan and Civil War History: In the Shadow of Grant and Sherman*. Kent, OH: Kent State University Press, 1998.

Sears, Stephen W. *To the Gates of Richmond: The Peninsula Campaign*. New York: Ticknor and Fields, 1992.

Sheehan-Dean, Aaron. *Why Confederates Fought: Family & Nation in Civil War Virginia*. Chapel Hill: University of North Carolina Press, 2007.

Shenandoah Valley Battlefields Foundation. *Shenandoah Valley Battlefields National Historic District: Final Management Plan*. New Market, VA: Shenandoah Valley Battlefields Foundation, 2000.

Simms, L. Moody, Jr. "Nineteenth Century Virginia Portraiture: Gennaro Persico, James W. Ford, and Louis M.D. Guillaume." *Southern Quarterly* 17, no 1 (1978): 15–28.

Stephenson, Richard W. "Jed Hotchkiss: Shenandoah Valley Mapmaker." *Winchester-Frederick County Historical Society Journal* 20 (2008–9): 43–57.

Stevenson, Lauralee Trent. *Confederate Soldier Artists: Painting the South's War*. Shippensburg, PA: White Mane Publishing, 1998.

Tanner, Robert G. *Stonewall in the Valley: Thomas J. "Stonewall" Jackson's Shenandoah Valley Campaign, Spring 1862*. Garden City, NY: Doubleday & Co., 1976.

Toomey, Daniel Carroll. *Hero at Front Royal: The Life of General John R. Kenly*. Baltimore, MD: Toomey Press, 2009.

Vandiver, Frank. *Mighty Stonewall: The Life and Campaigns of General Thomas Jackson*. College Station: Texas A&M University Press, 1957.

Wallenstein, Peter, and Bertram Wyatt-Brown, eds. *Virginia's Civil War*. Charlottesville: University of Virginia Press, 2005.

Williamson, Mrs. M.L. *The Life of Thomas J. Jackson, in Easy Words for the Young*. Richmond, VA: B.F. Johnson, 1899.

Wise, Jennings C. *The Military History of the Virginia Military Institute 1839 to 1865: With Appendix, Maps, and Illustrations*. N.p.: J.P. Bell Co., Inc., 1915.

Work, David. *Lincoln's Political Generals*. Urbana: University of Illinois Press, 2009.

# INDEX

# ABOUT THE AUTHOR

Jonathan A. Noyalas is an assistant professor of history and director of the Center for Civil War History at Lord Fairfax Community College in Middletown, Virginia, and the author or editor of seven books on Civil War–era history. Active in battlefield preservation, he serves on the board of directors of the Kernstown Battlefield Association and the committee  on interpretation and education of the Shenandoah Valley Battlefields Foundation. Professor Noyalas is currently serving as the Civil War historian for the historic resource study at Cedar Creek and Belle Grove National Historical Park.

Visit us at
www.historypress.net